Africa

Illustrators
Cheri Macoubrie Wilson
Wendy Chang
Mary E. Connors

Editor
Barbara Wally

Editorial Project Manager
Karen J. Goldfluss, M.S. Ed.

Editor-in-Chief:
Sharon Coan, M.S. Ed.

Creative Director
Elayne Roberts

Art Coordinator
Cheri Macoubrie Wilson

Cover Designer
Cheri Macoubrie Wilson

Product Manager
Phil Garcia

Imaging
James Edward Grace
Ralph Olmedo, Jr.

Publisher
Mary D. Smith, M.S. Ed.

Author

Barbara Gillespie-Washington

Teacher Created Resources, Inc.
6421 Industry Way
Westminster, CA 92683
www.teachercreated.com

©1999 Teacher Created Resources, Inc.
Reprinted, 2005
Made in U.S.A.

ISBN-1-57690-109-2

Table of Contents

Introduction

From Algeria to Zimbabwe, Africa, the second largest continent in the world, is a land of diversity and beauty. This book, *Africa,* provides an introduction to the land and people of Africa and the rich cultural heritage of the continent. Each of the five geographic regions of Africa has a unique environment contributing to the great diversity.

The African continent is so vast that we often limit our thinking to only one of the five geographic regions, like the savanna or the desert. The section north of the Sahara Desert includes the large countries of Egypt and Algeria. South of the great desert, countries like Ethiopia make up Eastern Africa, and Western Africa includes Nigeria and the Congo. Southern Africa is dominated by the large nation of South Africa. Madagascar and other islands are also part of Africa.

Africa is the site of the Sahara desert, which covers more than a quarter of the continent and is the largest desert on Earth. The desert is chiefly the domain of nomadic herders and their camels.

Savanna grasslands border the desert, providing a home for animals like the wildebeest, lions, zebras, and other intriguing animals. Many of these animals are unique to Africa. Along the equator, there are dense rain forests with thick, lush trees and undergrowth.

Anthropologists believe that people have lived in Africa longer than any other place in the world. In 1967 a fragment of a human jawbone was found in the eastern African country of Kenya. Estimated to be five million years old, this is considered the oldest human fragment ever found. Africa was the center of the earliest civilizations. Of all the ancient African cultures, the ancient Egyptian civilization is the best known. More than 5,000 years ago a powerful nation was built by the Egyptians along the Nile River. They built great cities and amazing pyramids, and they made incredible discoveries in math and medicine. Their culture continues to have a powerful influence on modern architecture and art throughout the world.

The rich African culture has touched the rest of the world in the stories, music, and traditions carried by African slaves to the Americas. Both jazz and gospel music grew from the deeply instilled African culture.

Early explorers sailed along the African coast and traded with various African peoples, but the continent remained unexplored until the mid-nineteenth century. Europeans who recognized the value of Africa's mineral wealth rushed to establish colonies on the "Dark Continent." The face of Africa has changed in recent years as native populations asserted their rights to self-rule and freedom from the European colonizers. The people of Africa continue to blend their cultural traditions with life in the modern world.

This unit was designed with the busy teacher in mind. An introduction to Africa's countries and regions as well as background information necessary to prepare and teach a unit about Africa have been provided for you. In addition to this unit's value as a reference tool, activity pages are provided to whet the curiosity of the student. The materials in this book are intended to whet the curiosity of the student. Each of the sections invites further study and innovation as you and your students explore Africa.

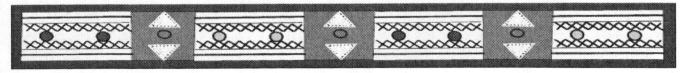

The Countries of Africa

This section serves as an introduction to the regions of Africa. Maps and general information about each country are provided for teacher or student use. If you wish to assign regional or country reports to groups of students or to individual students, the information and maps can be used to guide students toward further research. After students have researched their countries, have them complete the country report on pages 172-176. Encourage students to include additional pages and any relevant activities from this unit to their reports.

The Countries of Africa

Northern Africa

1. Algeria
2. Egypt
3. Libya
4. Morocco
5. Tunisia
6. Western Sahara

Eastern Africa

1. Burundi
2. Comoros
3. Djibouti
4. Eritrea
5. Ethiopia
6. Kenya
7. Madagascar
8. Mauritius
9. Rwanda
10. Seychelles
11. Somalia
12. Sudan
13. Tanzania
14. Uganda

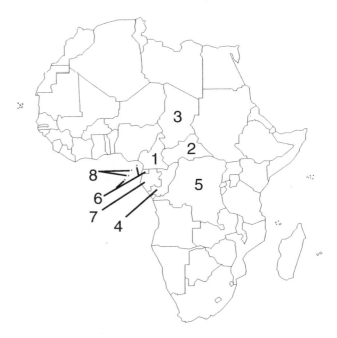

Central Africa

1. Cameroon
2. Central African Republic
3. Chad
4. Congo
5. Congo Republic
6. Equatorial Guinea
7. Gabon
8. São Tomé and Príncipe

The Countries of Africa *(cont.)*

Western Africa

1. Benin
2. Burkina Faso
3. Cape Verde
4. The Gambia
5. Ghana
6. Guinea
7. Guinea-Bissau
8. Côte d´ Ivoire
9. Liberia
10. Mali
11. Mauritania
12. Niger
13. Nigeria
14. Senegal
15. Sierra Leone
16. Togo

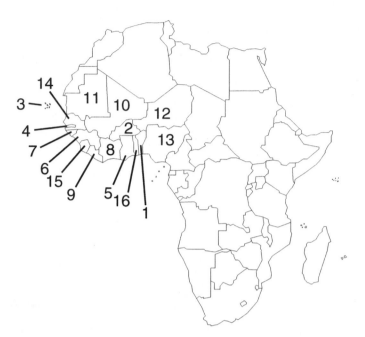

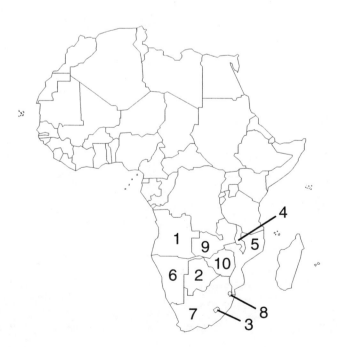

Southern Africa

1. Angola
2. Botswana
3. Lesotho
4. Malawi
5. Mozambique
6. Namibia
7. South Africa
8. Swaziland
9. Zambia
10. Zimbabwe

A Visit to Northern Africa

Northern Africa lies between the Mediterranean Sea and the Sahara desert. It includes the large countries of Egypt and Algeria. Since ancient times, this area has been influenced by European and Asian cultures. The peoples of this region include Berbers and Arabs.

Algeria

Democratic and Popular Republic of Algeria

Area in Square Miles: 919,595

Capital: Algiers

Climate: arid, semi-arid

Population in 1997: 29,830,370

Peoples of Algeria: over 90% Arab-Berber, some European

Major Languages Spoken in Algeria: Arabic, Berber dialects, French

Religions Practiced in Algeria: Sunni Muslim, Christian, traditional indigenous

Currency in 1997: 59.64 Algerian dinars = $1.00 U.S.

Natural Resources: crude oil, natural gas, iron ore, phosphates, uranium, lead, zinc

Agriculture: citrus fruits, olives, grapes, dates, tobacco, barley, wheat, oats, cattle, sheep

Industry: oil production, agriculture

Interesting Facts: Beginning in 1830 Algeria was a colony of France. In 1962, following fierce battles between the French colonists and Algerians, Algeria won independence. Algeria is one of the largest countries in Africa. Most of the country is covered by the Sahara desert. Over 90% of the population lives within 200 miles of the Mediterranean Sea. Over 43% of the population lives in crowded coastal cities.

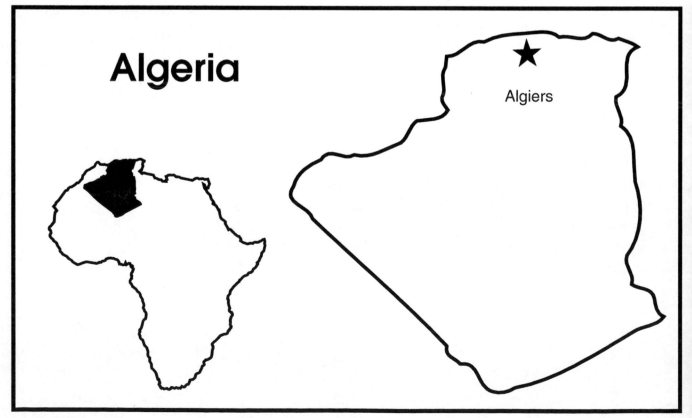

Algeria

Algiers

Egypt
Arab Republic of Egypt

Area in Square Miles: 385,229

Capital: Cairo

Climate: arid, semi-arid

Population in 1997: 64,791,891

Peoples of Egypt: 90% Hamitic, others: Greek, Italian, Syro-Lebanese

Major Languages Spoken in Egypt: Arabic, English, French

Religions Practiced in Egypt: Muslim, Coptic Christian

Currency in 1997: 3.4 Egyptian pounds = $1.00 U.S.

Natural Resources: crude oil, natural gas, iron ore, phosphates, manganese, limestone, gypsum, talc, asbestos, lead, zinc

Agriculture: cotton, datepalms, sugarcane, rice, barley, maize

Industry: oil production, ironworks, mining, textiles, tourism

Interesting Facts: Egypt gained independence from the British in 1952. Egypt is the home of the ancient civilization of the Pharaohs. Today tourists and scholars from around the globe visit and study the famous pyramids and sphinx. Over 95% of the Egyptian population lives near the fertile banks of the Nile River. Egyptians trade by ship across the Red Sea and the Mediterranean Sea. Egypt is one of the most populated countries in Africa, and a shortage of farmland causes the government to import food.

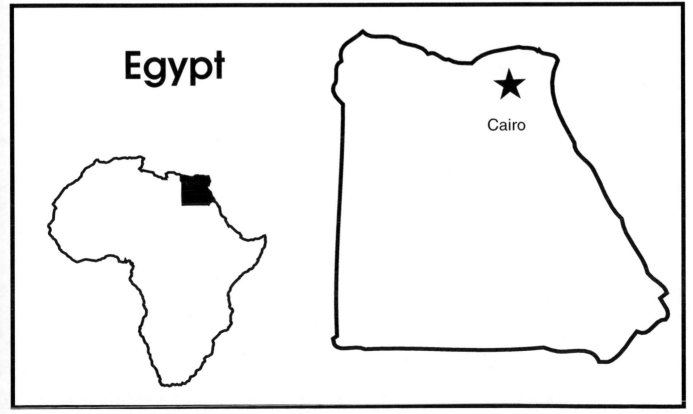

Egypt

Cairo

Libya

Socialist People's Libyan Arab Jamahiriya

Area in Square Miles: 679,359

Capital: Tripoli

Climate: Mediterranean coast, arid

Population in 1997: 5,648,359

Peoples of Lybia: Over 90% Berber and Arab, others: European, Asian

Major Languages Spoken in Libya: Arabic, Italian, English

Religions Practiced in Libya: Muslim, Christian

Currency in 1997: 0.38 Libyan dinars = $1.00 U.S.

Natural Resources: crude oil, natural gas, gypsum

Agriculture: dates, barley, olives, wheat, peanuts, tobacco

Industry: oil and gas production, mining

Interesting Facts: Libya gained independence from the Italians in 1951. Over 90% of the population lives within 200 miles of the Mediterranean Sea. Libya is the richest country in Africa due to its oil reserves. Libya is one of the largest countries in Africa, but most of the land is barren Saharan desert. Therefore, Libya must import over 75% of its food from other countries that have more farmland and rainfall. Part of the early empire of Carthage was in the land that is now called Libya.

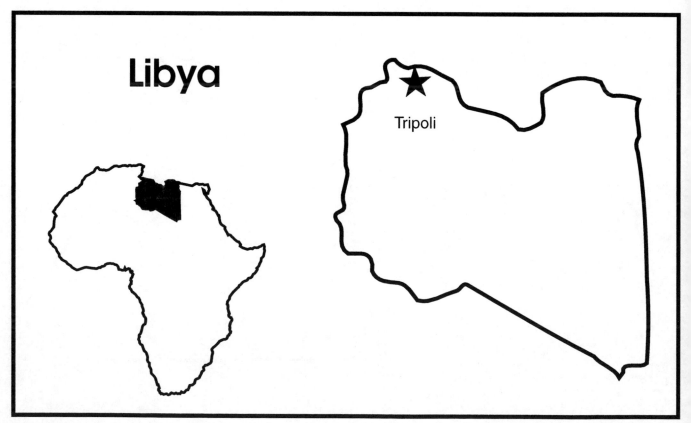

Libya

Tripoli

Morocco

Kingdom of Morocco

Area in Square Miles: 177,117

Capital: Rabat

Climate: semi-arid, arid

Population in 1997: 30,391,423

Peoples of Morocco: over 90% Arab-Berber, others: European, Jewish

Major Languages Spoken in Morocco: Arabic, French, Spanish, Berber dialects

Religions Practiced in Morocco: over 90% Muslim, others: Jewish, Christian

Currency in 1997: 9.77 Moroccan dirhams = $1.00 U.S.

Natural Resources: phosphates, iron ore, manganese, lead, zinc

Agriculture: phosphate production, mining, tourism, carpets, clothing

Interesting Facts: France and Spain partitioned Morocco in 1912. Morocco gained independence in 1956 and is ruled today by King Hassan II. Over 90% of the large population live near the Atlantic Coast. Fez is an ancient city that was once the center of an Islamic empire. Merchants from Morocco continue to trade on camel caravans across the Sahara desert. The Atlas Mountains separate southern Morocco from the desert. Morocco is famous for woven textile arts, silks, leatherwork and colorful tiled architecture. The early Greeks called Morocco the "Garden of the Gods" because of the many flowers and natural beauty of the landscape.

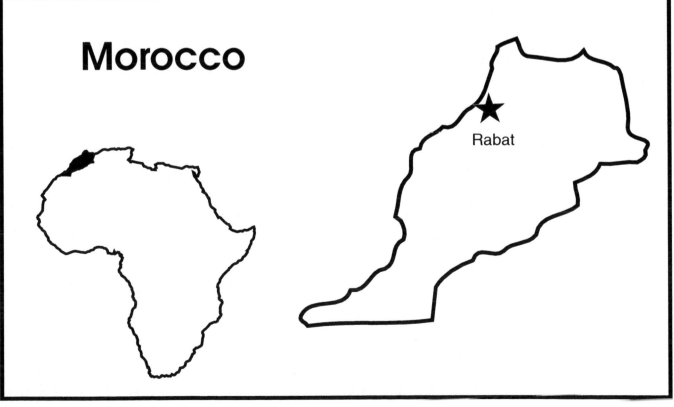

Morocco

Rabat

Tunisia

Republic of Tunisia

Area in Square Miles: 63,170

Capital: Tunis

Climate: Mediterranean coast, arid interior

Population in 1997: 9,183,097

Peoples of Tunisia: over 90% Arab-Berber, others: Jewish, European

Major Languages Spoken in Tunisia: Arabic, French

Religions Practiced in Tunisia: over 90% Muslim, others: Jewish, Christian

Currency in 1997: 1.21 Tunisian dinars = $1.00 U.S.

Natural Resources: crude oil, phosphates, iron ore, lead, zinc, salt

Agriculture: citrus fruits, olives, grapes, dates

Industry: oil production, food processing, textiles, mining

Interesting Facts: The French occupied Tunisia from 1881 to 1956, when Tunisia gained its independence. The land of Tunisia is mostly Sahara desert. Over 90% of the population lives within 200 miles of the Mediterranean Sea. About half of the population lives in cities. In 146 B.C. Tunisia was part of the Empire of Carthage. The early Empire of Sudan once claimed Tunisian land. Today many Europeans visit Tunisia to enjoy the beautiful coastal areas. Merchants of Tunisia continue to trade as they always have across the Mediterranean Sea.

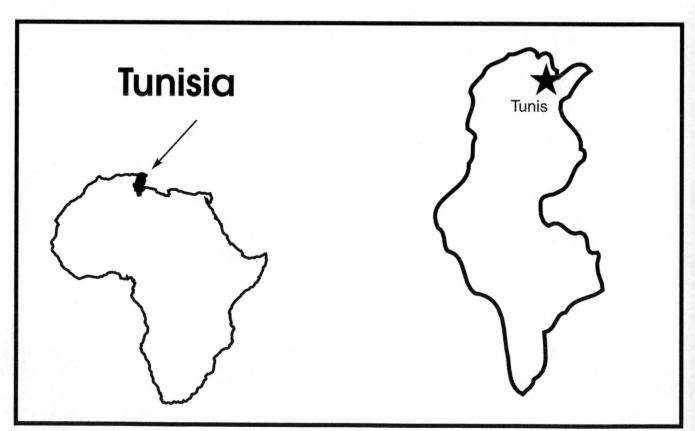

Western Sahara

Area in Square Miles: 102,703

Capital: none

Climate: semi-arid, arid

Population in 1995: 217,211

Peoples of Western Sahara: over 90% Arab, Berber

Major Languages Spoken in Western Sahara: Arabic, Berber dialects

Religions Practiced in Western Sahara: over 90% Muslim

Currency in 1995: 9.89 Moroccan dirhams = $1.00 U.S.

Natural Resources: phosphates, iron ore

Agriculture: citrus fruits, olives, grapes, camels, sheep, goats, barley, fishing, date palms

Industry: phosphate

Interesting Facts: The land area of Western Sahara was formerly divided between Morocco in the northern area and Mauritania in the southern area. In 1991, a Unitied Nations cease-fire brought an end to the years of fighting between many groups. The exact boundaries and legal status of this country are still in dispute. Western Sahara is largely barren desert and only a small amount of land is suitable for agriculture. There are few natural resources here so the population must depend on Morocco for food.

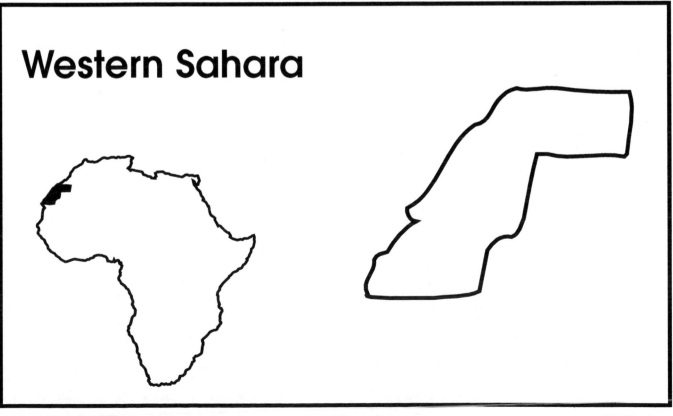

Western Sahara

A Visit to Western Africa

Western Africa is part of the Low Africa land region. It primarily consists of forest and grasslands. The annual rainfall averages in parts of western Africa are as much as 100 inches (250 cm). Land in western Africa is primarily used for subsistence farming with coastal patches of forest land production.

Benin

People's Republic of Benin

Area in Square Miles: 43,483

Capital: Porto-Novo

Climate: tropical

Population in 1997: 5,902,178

Peoples of Benin: Fon, Adja, Yoruba, Bariba, European

Major Languages Spoken in Benin: French Fon, Yoruba, Adja, Bariba

Religions Practiced in Benin: traditional indigenous, Muslim, Christian

Currency in 1997: 610 CFA francs = $1.00 U.S.

Natural Resources: farmland

Agriculture: palm products, cotton, corn, yams, cassava, cocoa, coffee, groundnuts

Industry: shoes, beer, textiles, cement, processing palm oil

Interesting Facts: From 1892 to 1960 the French ruled Benin as a colony. Benin was called "Dahomey" until 1975. The Fon people, who are known for their appliquéd cloths, established the famous Dahomey kingdom. Benin has always been a trade corridor between the savanna regions of Western Africa and the coast. Benin is known for fine sculptures of ivory and bronze. The leopard is the symbol of royalty in Benin.

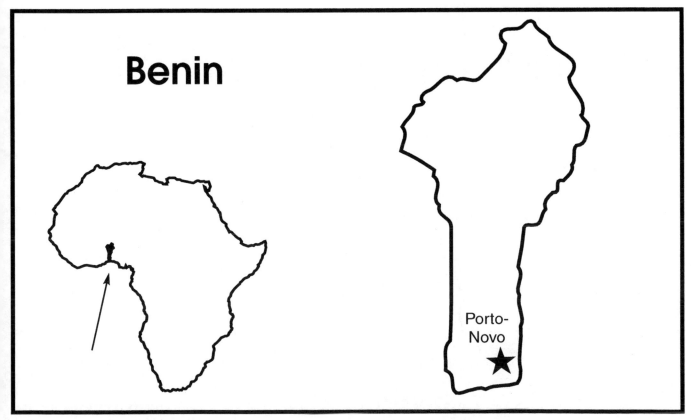

Benin

Porto-Novo ★

Burkina Faso

Area in Square Miles: 106,000

Capital: Ouagadougou

Climate: tropical to arid

Population in 1997: 10,891,159

Peoples of Burkina Faso: Mossi, Burunsi, Senufo, Lobi, Bobo, Mande, Fulani

Major Languages Spoken in Burkina Faso: Portuguese, Kriolo, Fula, Manjaca, Mandika

Religions Practiced in Burkina Faso: traditional indigenous, Muslim, Christian

Currency in 1997: 610 CFA francs = $1.00 U.S.

Natural Resources: manganese, limestone, marble, gold, uranium, bauxite, copper

Agriculture: millet, sorghum, corn, rice, livestock, peanuts, shea nuts, sugarcane, cotton, sesame

Industry: soft drinks, agricultural processing, brewing

Interesting Facts: From 1896 to 1960 Burkina Faso was a French colony. Until 1966, the name of Burkina Faso was the Republic of Upper Volta. The great Mossi kingdom was formed in 1313 and is known for fine arts. Traditional homes are often painted by women with bright colors and geometrical patterns. This country is known for its modern film industry. Recent droughts have caused hardship on the herders and others.

Burkina Faso

Ouagadougou
★

Cape Verde

Republic of Cape Verde

Area in Square Miles: 1,557

Capital: Praia

Climate: temperate, marine

Population in 1997: 393,843

Peoples of Cape Verde: Creole, African, European

Major Languages Spoken in Cape Verde: Portuguese, Kriolu

Religions Practiced in Cape Verde: Catholic, traditional indigenous

Currency in 1997: 96.59 escudos = $1.00 U.S.

Natural Resources: fish, agricultural land, salt deposits

Agriculture: corn, beans, manioc, sweet potatoes, bananas

Industry: fishing, flour mills, salt

Interesting Facts: Cape Verde gained independence from the Portuguese in 1975. Bananas are the only export crop. Cape Verde has a rich tradition of music, dance, poetry, and storytelling. Riddles and proverbs are popular with children and adults. The government is now promoting the offshore islands of Cape Verde for tourism and as special banking centers.

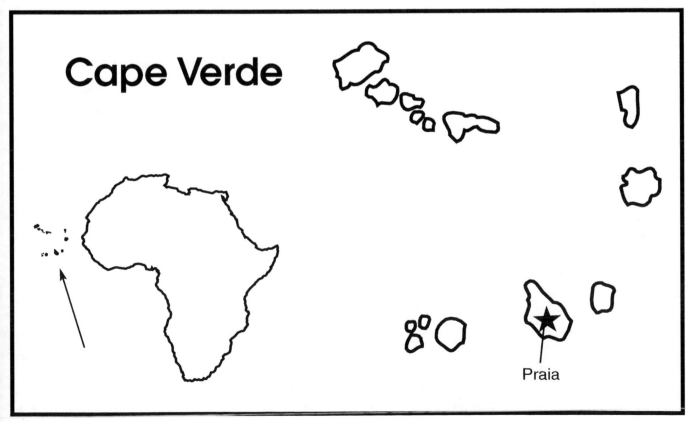

Praia

Côte d'Ivoire

Republic of Ivory Coast

Area in Square Miles: 124,503

Capital: Abidjan (de facto), Yamoussoukro (official)

Climate: tropical

Population in 1997: 14,986,218

Peoples of Côte d'Ivoire: Baoule, Bete, Senoufou, Malinke, others

Major Languages Spoken in Côte d'Ivoire: French, Dioula, Agni, Baoule, Kru, Senoufo

Religions Practiced in Côte d'Ivoire: Muslim, traditional indigenous, Christian

Currency in 1997: 610 CFA francs = $1.00 U.S.

Natural Resources: timber, agricultural lands

Agriculture: cotton, coffee, bananas, pineapples, corn, millet, pineapples, rubber, palm oil

Industry: food and lumber processing, textiles, oil refinery, soap, car assembly

Interesting Facts: A French colony from 1893 to 1960, Côte d'Ivoire is well known for the beauty and grace of its art. The Dan, Senoufo, and Baoule peoples carve masks and figures of humans and animals from wood. The Dan masks are used in ritual dance celebrations. Other great arts of Côte d'Ivoire include music and textile weavings of bright colors.

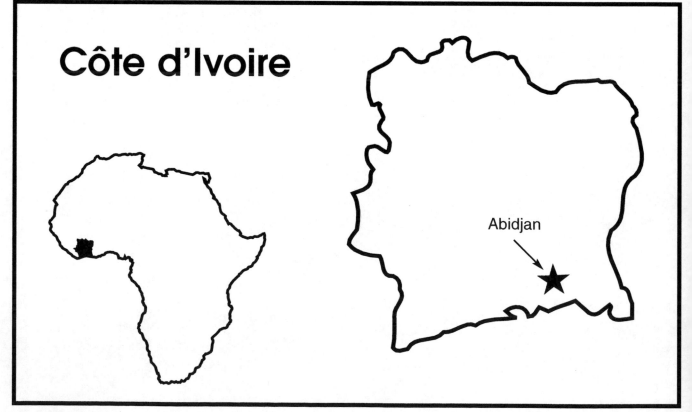

Côte d'Ivoire

Abidjan

The Gambia

Republic of The Gambia

Area in Square Miles: 4,361

Capital: Banjul

Climate: subtropical

Population in 1997: 1,248,085

Peoples of Gambia: Mandinka, Fula, Wolof, others

Major Languages Spoken in Gambia: English, Mandinka, Wolof, Fula, Sarakola, Diula

Religions Practiced in Gambia: Muslim, Christian, traditional indigenous

Currency in 1997: 10.46 dalasis = $1.00 U.S.

Natural Resources: fish, ilmenite, zircon, rutile

Agriculture: cotton, sorghum, fish, peanuts, millet, livestock

Industry: peanuts, soft drinks, agricultural machinery assembly, clothing, tourism, wood and metalworking

Interesting Facts: From 1807 to 1965 Gambia was a colony of Great Britain. Gambia is a narrow country that lies along the great Gambia River. The country juts into the country of Senegal. The American author Alex Haley wrote the book *Roots* about his search for his African relatives in Gambia. Many tourists visit this country after reading Haley's book.

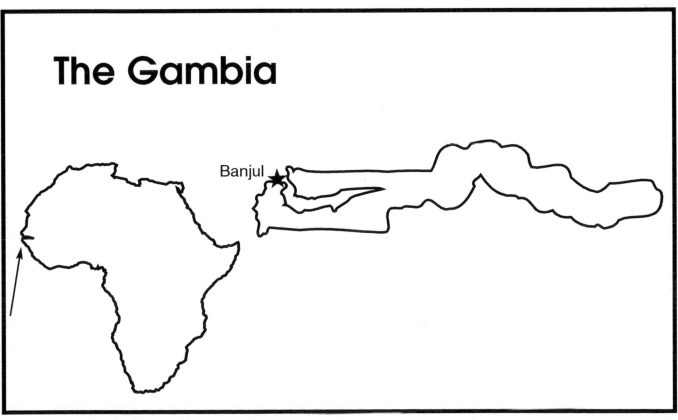

The Gambia

Banjul

Ghana
Republic of Ghana

Area in Square Miles: 92,100

Capital: Accra

Climate: tropical to semi-arid

Population in 1997: 18,100,703

Peoples of Ghana: Akan, Moshi-Dagomba, Ewe, Ga, others

Major Languages Spoken in Ghana: English, Akan, Ewe, Asante, Hausa, Ga, Twi

Religions Practiced in Ghana: traditional indigenous, Muslim, Christian

Currency in 1997: 2,190 cedis = $1.00 U.S.

Natural Resources: gold, diamonds, fish, timber, oil, bauxite, manganese

Agriculture: cocoa, coconuts, coffee, rubber

Industry: mining, lumber, fishing, aluminum

Interesting Facts: Ghana was a colony of Great Britain from 1901 to 1957. Ghana is the home of the Asante people, who are well known for their gold jewelry and colorful woven textiles, such as the kente cloth. There was so much gold mined in this country that the currency of the Asante was once gold dust. This dust was weighed on scales with gold weights. Fishing is done with nets in the rivers and coastal waters of Ghana. Music and song are very popular in Ghana.

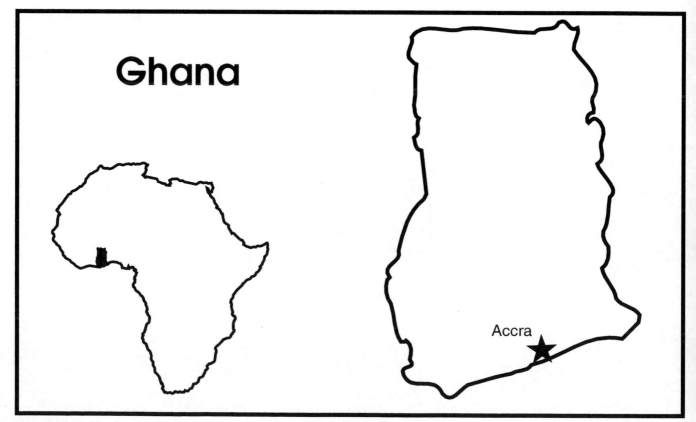

Ghana

Accra

Guinea
Republic of Guinea

Area in Square Miles: 94,926

Capital: Conakry

Climate: tropical

Population in 1997: 7,405,375

Peoples of Guinea: Peuhl, Malinke, Soussou, other tribes

Major Languages Spoken in Guinea: French, Soussou, Peuhl, Malinke

Religions Practiced in Guinea: Muslim, Christian

Currency in 1997: 1,119 francs = $1.00 U.S.

Natural Resources: bauxite, iron, diamonds, gold

Agriculture: bananas, pineapples, rice, palm kernels, coffee, cassava

Industry: mining, light manufacturing, agricultural processing

Interesting Facts: Guinea was under French control during 1849 and became a French colony in 1891. It gained independence from French influence in 1958. Guinea has had a history of civil and political unrest until recent years.

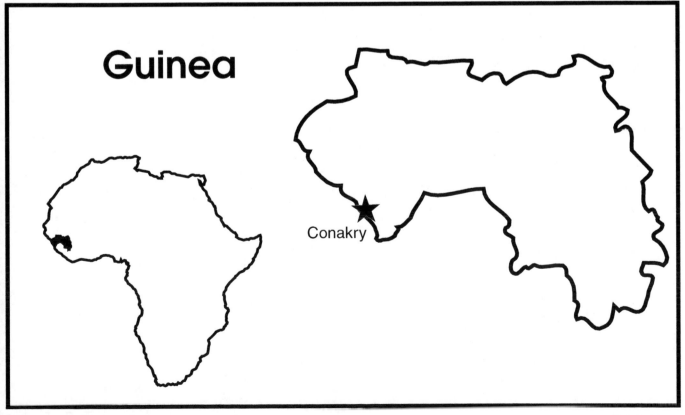

Guinea

Conakry

Guinea-Bissau
Republic of Guinea-Bissau

Area in Square Miles: 13,948

Capital: Bissau

Climate: tropical

Population in 1997: 1,178,584

Peoples of Guinea-Bissau: Balanta, Fula, Manjaca, Mandinga, others

Major Languages Spoken in Guinea-Bissau: Portuguese, Criolo, Fula, Manjaca, Mandinga

Religions Practiced in Guinea-Bissau: traditional indigenous, Muslim, Christian

Currency in 1997: 610 francs = $1.00 U.S.

Natural Resources: timber, shrimp, fish, bauxite

Agriculture: rice, peanuts, palm kernels, groundnuts, cotton

Industry: soft drinks, agricultural processing, beer, animal hides

Interesting Facts: From 1915 to 1974 Guinea-Bissau was controlled by Portugal. There are 40 small islands called the Bijagos Archipelago near the coast of Guinea-Bissau. The government of Guinea-Bissau wants to develop these islands for tourism as a way to earn money for the country's economy. This country needs to import food to help feed the growing population. Fishing is often done with nets and canoes by men and boys.

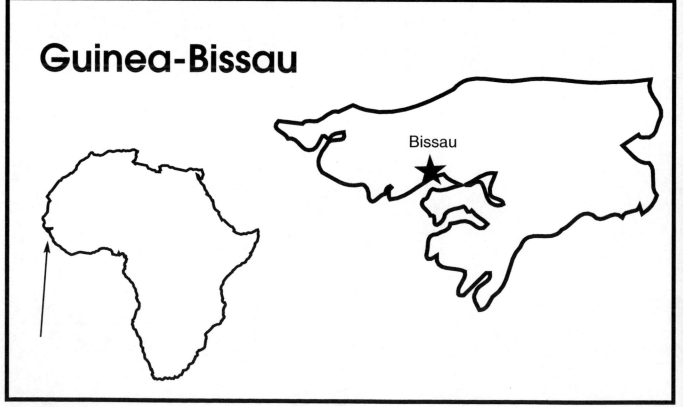

Guinea-Bissau

Bissau

Liberia

Republic of Liberia

Area in Square Miles: 43,000

Capital: Monrovia

Climate: tropical

Population in 1997: 2,602,068

Peoples of Liberia: Americo-Liberians, indigenous Africans

Major Languages Spoken in Liberia: English, Kriolo, Fula, Manjaca, Mandika

Religions Practiced in Liberia: traditional indigenous, Muslim, Christian

Currency in 1997: 1 Liberian dollar = $1.00 U.S.

Natural Resources: timber, iron ore, rubber, diamonds

Agriculture: rice, palm oil, cassava, sugar, coffee, cocoa, rubber

Industry: rubber processing, food processing, lumbermilling, iron and diamond mining

Interesting Facts: In 1822 African American settlers formed a government in Liberia. Liberia was never colonized by a European nation. Many Liberians want to have a government based on democracy. Most of the cities are found along the Atlantic Ocean coast. Fishing boats and trade ships are a common sight here.

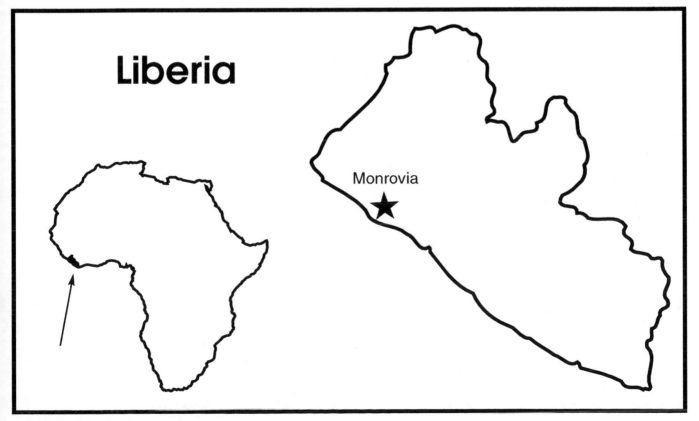

Liberia

Monrovia

Mali

Republic of Mali

Area in Square Miles: 478,819

Capital: Bamako

Climate: tropical to arid

Population in 1997: 9,945,383

Peoples of Mali: Turaneg, Moor, Bambara, Fulani (Peul), Soninke, Malinke

Major Languages Spoken in Mali: French, Bambara, Malinke, Bwa, Tamacheg, Dogon, Ful, Songhaic Arabic

Religions Practiced in Mali: Muslim, traditional indigenous, Christian

Currency in 1997: 610 CFA francs = $1.00 U.S.

Natural Resources: bauxite, iron ore, manganese, lithium, phosphate, kaolin, salt, limestone, gold

Agriculture: millet, sorghum, corn, rice sugar, cotton, peanuts, livestock

Industry: food processing, textiles, cigarettes, fishing

Interesting Facts: The country now known as Mali was a French colony from 1890 to 1960. From the fourth to the thirteenth centuries, the ancient empire of Ghana (which is not the same as modern-day Ghana) ruled Mali and exported gold to Asia, Europe, and other African countries. The great empire of Mali was founded over 600 years ago by the hero-king Sundiata Keita. The empire of Songhai later ruled until the sixteenth century. Timbuktu was once the center for trade and Islamic learning. Timbuktu is still used for trade by camel caravans crossing the Sahara desert. The unique mosque of Djenne is built of wood and clay. Mali is known for its puppet theaters and fine arts.

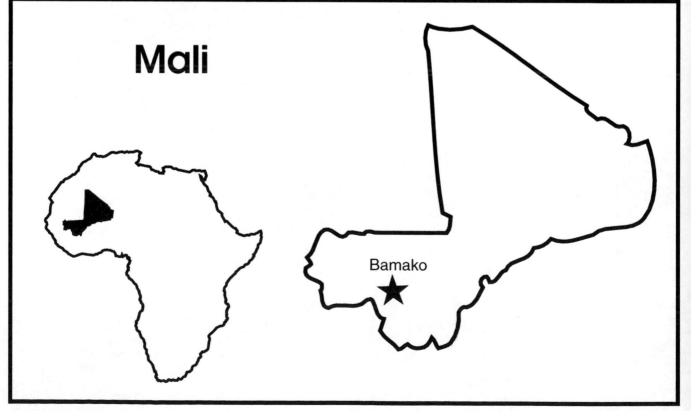

Mauritania

Islamic Republic of Mauritania

Area in Square Miles: 398,000

Capital: Nouakchott

Climate: arid to semi-arid

Population in 1997: 2,411,317

Peoples of Mauritania: Maur, Berber, African, others

Major Languages Spoken in Mauritania: Arabic, French, Hassaniyah, Fulfulde, Berber languages

Religions Practices in Mauritania: Muslim

Currency in 1997: 155 ouguiyas = $1.00 U.S.

Natural Resources: iron ore, gypsum, fish, copper

Agriculture: millet, corn, livestock, wheat, dates, rice, peanuts

Industry: iron-ore mining, fish processing

Interesting Facts: In 1960 Mauritania gained independence from France. There is only one major road in this country. Most of the land is desert, and water is scarce. Fine textiles and silver jewelry are made in Mauritania. Camels are often used for travel and for the transport of goods across the hot desert. Some homes are painted inside and outside with colorful designs.

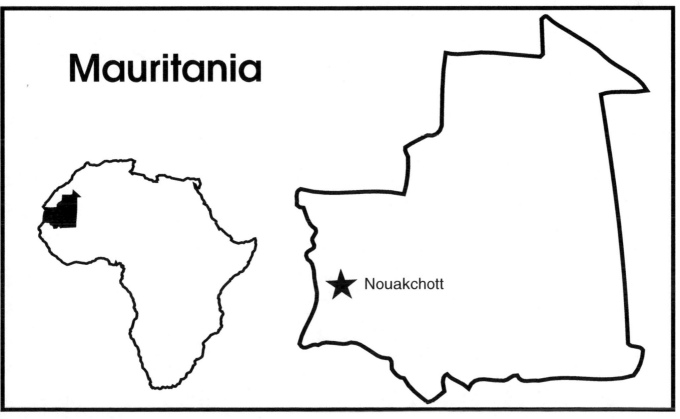

Mauritania

★ Nouakchott

Niger

Republic of Niger

Area in Square Miles: 489,191

Capital: Niamey

Climate: arid to semi-arid

Population in 1997: 9,388,859

Peoples of Niger: Hausa, Djerma, Fula, Tuareg, others

Major Languages Spoken in Niger: French, Hausa, Songhai, Fulde, Kanuri

Religions Practiced in Niger: Muslim, traditional indigenous, Christian

Currency in 1997: 610 CFA francs = $1.00 U.S.

Natural Resources: iron, phosphates, coal, tin, uranium

Agriculture: cotton, beans, sorghum, peanuts, millet

Industry: cement, textiles, mining, agricultural products

Interesting Facts: From 1906 to 1960 France governed Niger as a colony. The great Mali empire, which ruled about 800 years ago, included areas of present-day Niger. Tuareg nomads now live in the deserts of Niger. Many trees are planted each year to hold back the desert sands which spread out farther each year. People must often travel for miles to find water here. Even with the invention of trucks and airplanes, camels are still commonly used for travel and the transport of trade goods. Horses are highly prized symbols of wealth.

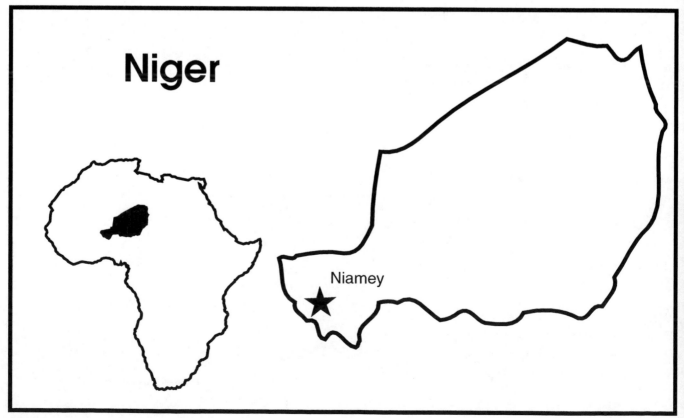

Niger

Niamey

Nigeria

Federal Republic of Nigeria

Area in Square Miles: 356,669

Capital: Abuja

Climate: arid to tropical

Population in 1997: 107,129,469

Peoples of Nigeria: Hausa, Yoruba, Ibo, Fulani, others

Major Languages Spoken in Nigeria: English, Hausa, Yoruba, Igbo, Efik, Idoma

Religions Practiced in Nigeria: Muslim, traditional indigenous, Christian

Currency in 1997: 85.20 nairas = $1.00 U.S.

Natural Resources: oil, timber, minerals

Agriculture: cotton, rubber, cocoa, cassava, yams, sorghum

Industry: mining, natural gas, coal, cotton, rubber, textiles, cement

Interesting Facts: From 1851 to 1960 Nigeria was a colony of the British. Nigeria is well known for its arts such as sculpture. Many great authors, such as Nobel laureate Wole Soyinka, come from Nigeria. Many of the Africans who were brought to America during the slave trade were from Nigeria.

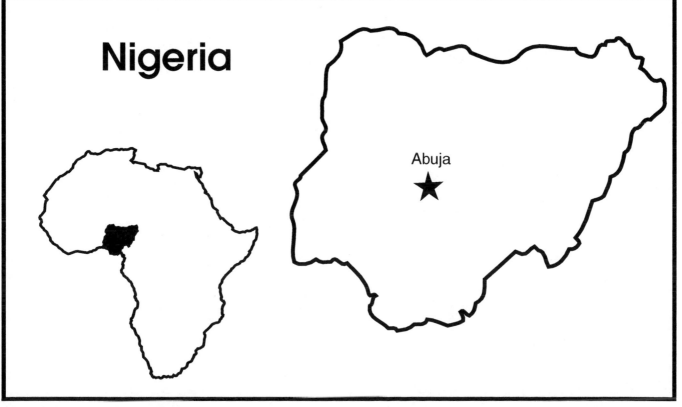

Nigeria

Abuja ★

Senegal

Republic of Senegal

Area in Square Miles: 76,000

Capital: Dakar

Climate: tropical

Population in 1997: 9,403,546

Peoples of Senegal: Wolof, Fulani, Serer, Toucouleur, Diola, Mandingo, others

Major Languages Spoken in Senegal: French, Wolof, Fulde, Oyola, Maningo, Sarakole, Serer

Religions Practiced in Senegal: Muslim, traditional indigenous, Christian

Currency in 1997: 610 CFA francs = $1.00 U.S.

Natural Resources: fish, phosphates

Agriculture: millet, sorghum, manioc, rice, cotton, groundnuts

Industry: fishing, food processing, light manufacturing

Interesting Facts: In 1960 Senegal gained independence from France. During the colonial period, the small island of Goree near Dakkar was the center for the Atlantic slave trade by the Dutch, French, and English. Over 90% of the Senegalese are now Muslim. Large mosques are found in every city. The Senegal River is one of the great rivers of Africa and is important for fishing and trade.

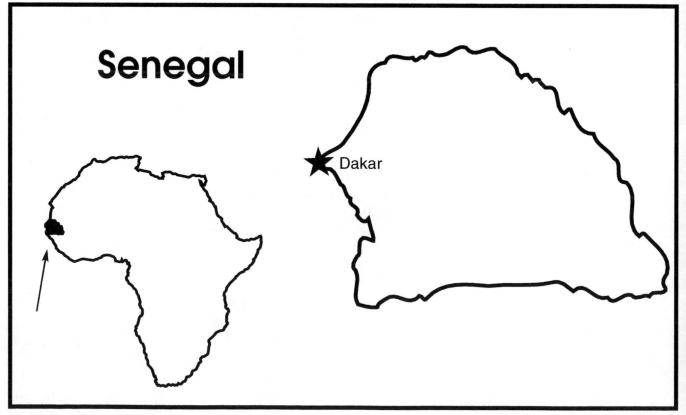

Senegal

Dakar

Sierra Leone

Republic of Sierra Leone

Area in Square Miles: 27,925

Capital: Freetown

Climate: tropical

Population in 1997: 4,891,546

Peoples of Sierra Leone: Temne, Mende, Krio, others

Major Languages Spoken in Sierra Leone: English, Krio, Temne, Mende, Vai, Kru, Fulde

Religions Practiced in Sierra Leone: traditional indigenous, Muslim, Christian

Currency in 1997: 863 leones = $1.00 U.S.

Natural Resources: diamonds, bauxite, rutile, iron ore, chromite

Agriculture: coffee, cocoa, ginger, rice, piassava, bananas, fish

Industry: mining, beverages, cigarettes, construction materials

Interesting Facts: In 1961 Sierra Leone gained independence from Britain. Sierra Leone is known for bright textiles. Trade ships are a common sight upon the coastal waters. Sierra Leone has mountains and lush forests. The name Sierra Leone means "sleeping lion" because the mountain range looks like a lion taking a nap. The seaports of Sierra Leone are part of the international trading routes of Africa. Trade partners include Japan, China, America, and Nigeria.

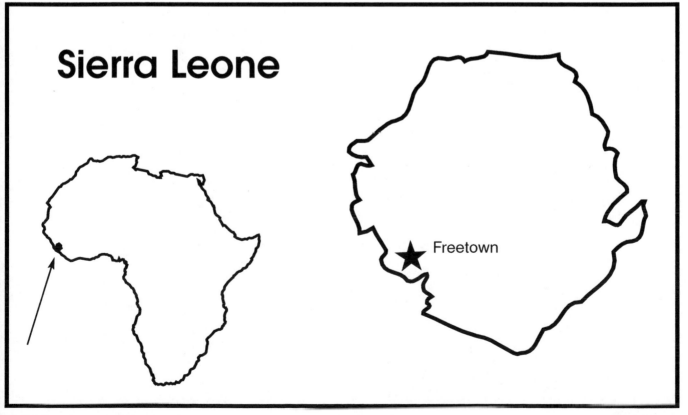

Sierra Leone

Freetown

Togo
Republic of Togo

Area in Square Miles: 21,622

Capital: Lome

Climate: tropical to arid

Population in 1997: 4,735,610

Peoples of Togo: Ewe, Mina, Kabye, some European and Syrian-Lebanese

Major Languages Spoken in Togo: French, Ewe, Mina, Dagomba, Kabye

Religions Practiced in Togo: traditional indigenous, Christian, Muslim

Currency in 1997: 610 CFA francs = $1.00 U.S.

Natural Resources: marble, limestone, phosphates

Agriculture: coffee, cotton, cocoa, yams cassava, corn, beans, rice, sorghum, millet, fishing, some livestock

Industry: phosphate mining, agricultural processing, cement, handicrafts, textiles, beverages

Interesting Facts: Togo gained independence from France in 1960. The terrain has hills, rolling savanna, and a low coastal plain with lagoons and swampy marshes. Most of the population are farmers. This country is able to grow all the food that they need. Togo is a commercial and trade center for western Africa. Boats have traded at the Atlantic coastline ports of Togo for many generations.

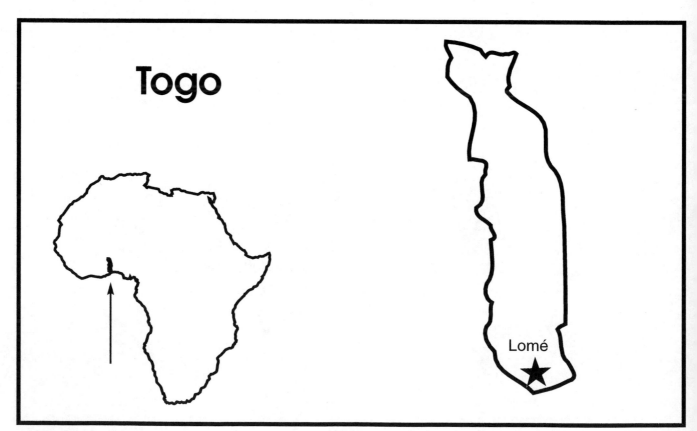

A Visit to Central Africa

As part of the Low Africa land region, central Africa is covered with dense tropical rain forests. The average rainfall in this region ranges from 10–80 inches (25–203 cm), and the regional climate various from semi-arid to tropical wet. Land in central Africa is primarily used for subsistence farming, grazing, and some forest land production. Some of chief agricultural products of this region are millet, cotton, coffee, cacao, and cassava.

Cameroon

Republic of Cameroon

Area in Square Miles: 183,568

Capital: Yaounde

Climate: equatorial, tropical rain forest

Population in 1997: 14,677,510

Peoples of Cameroon: Bantu, Fang, Bamileke, Duala, Kirdi, Fulani, others

Major Languages Spoken in Cameroon: French, Lingala, Kikongo, English, others

Religions Practiced in Cameroon: Christian, traditional indigenous, Muslim

Currency in 1997: 610 CFA francs = $1.00 U.S.

Natural Resources: crude oil, bauxite, iron ore, timber

Agriculture: coffee, cocoa, timber, cotton, rubber, bananas, palm oil, oilseed, grains, livestock, roots and tubers

Industry: crude oil products, aluminum plant, sawmills, food processing

Interesting Facts: Cameroon gained independence from the French in the year 1960. Trade and travel take place on the large rivers which flow towards the Atlantic Ocean. Because over half of the land is dense rain forest and difficult to clear, most people live on the coastline and along existing railroad lines. Artisans in Cameroon produce traditional wooden sculptures and objects for sale to tourists.

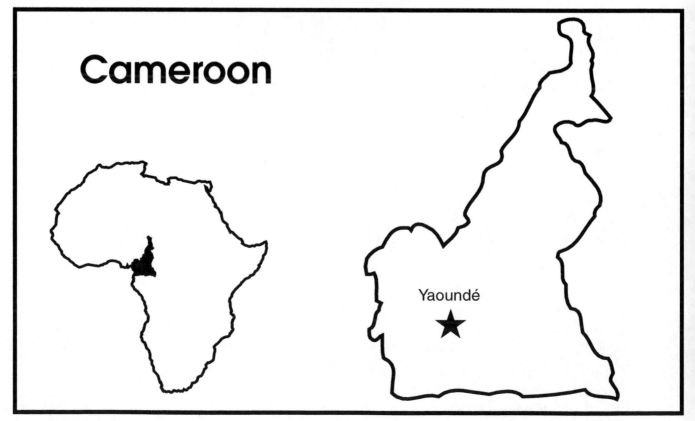

Cameroon

Yaoundé

Central African Republic
C.A.R.

Area in Square Miles: 240,324

Capital: Bangui

Climate: tropical to semi-arid

Population in 1997: 3,342,051

Peoples of Central African Republic: Banda, Baya, Mandjia, Sara, others

Major Languages Spoken in Central African Republic: French, Sango, Baya, Mandjia

Religions Practiced in Central African Republic: traditional indigenous, Roman Catholic, Protestant, Muslim

Currency in 1997: 610 CFA francs = $1.00 U.S.

Natural Resources: diamonds, uranium, timber

Agriculture: coffee, cotton, peanuts, food crops, livestock

Industry: timber, textiles, soap, cigarettes, processed food, diamond mining

Interesting Facts: In 1960 the Central African Republic gained independence from France. France is still involved in the economy and politics of this country. Most of the cities of C.A.R. are found along the rivers. Other cities are on the savanna grasslands. Many families herd cattle and lead their animals to water and fresh grazing land. This country is mostly self-sufficient in food production. Important trading partners include France, Belgium, Italy, Japan, and America.

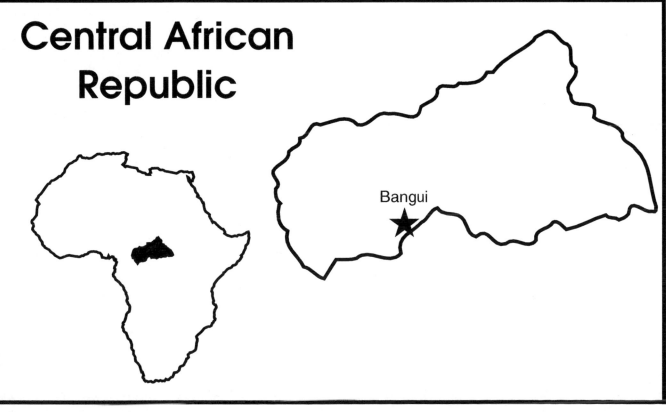

Central African Republic

Bangui

Chad

Republic of Chad

Area in Square Miles: 496,000

Capital: N'Djamena

Climate: arid, tropical

Population in 1997: 7,166,023

Peoples of Chad: 200 distinct groups

Major Languages Spoken in Chad: French, Chadian, Arabic, Fulde, Hausa, Kotoko, Kanembou, Sara Maba, others

Religions Practiced in Chad: Muslim, Christian, traditional indigenous

Currency in 1997: 610 CFA francs = $1.00 U.S.

Natural Resources: petroleum, uranium, natron, kaolin

Agriculture: cotton, cattle, fish, sugar

Industry: livestock, beer, textiles, cigarettes, bicycle and radio assembly

Interesting Facts: In 1960 Chad gained independence from France. Chad is divided into three climatic zones—the southern savanna, the middle Sahel area, and the northern Sahara desert. Lake Chad provides water for farming and livestock production. The peoples of each region follow different lifestyles and customs. The present government is trying to unify the country to improve land management, agriculture, and other industry options.

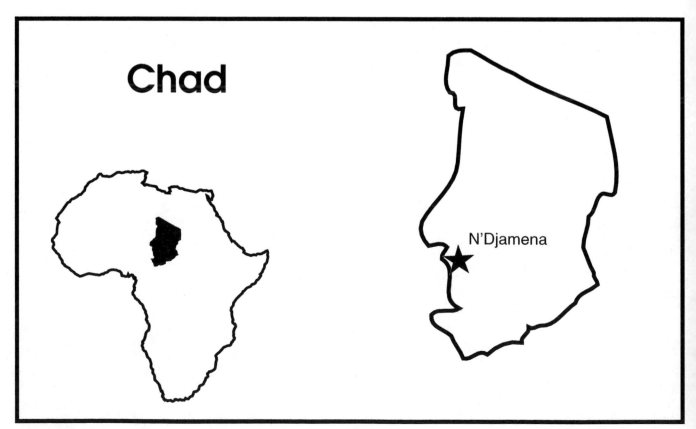

Chad

N'Djamena

Congo

Democratic Republic of the Congo (formerly Zaire)

Area in Square Miles: 905,500

Capital: Kinshasa

Climate: hot, humid, equatorial

Population in 1997: 47,440,362

Peoples of Congo: Bantu majority, over 200 African groups

Major Languages Spoken in Congo: Swahili, French, Lingala, Luba, others

Religious Practice in Congo: traditional indigenous, Christian, Muslim

Currency in 1997: 2.50 Congolese francs = $1.00 U.S.

Natural Resources: copper, cobalt, diamonds, zinc, gold, manganese, tin, bauxite, iron, coal, timber

Agriculture: coffee, rubber, palm oil, tea, cotton, cocoa, manoic, bananas, corn, plantains, rice, sugar

Industry: mineral mining, food processing, consumer products, cement

Interesting Facts: The Congo was formerly known as the Belgium Congo during the European colonial period. This country has great mineral wealth and fertile farmland with adequate rainfall. However, the Congo remains one of the poorest countries in the world. It is one-quarter the size of the United States. Trading partners include Belgium, France, Germany, America, Italy, Japan, and Britain.

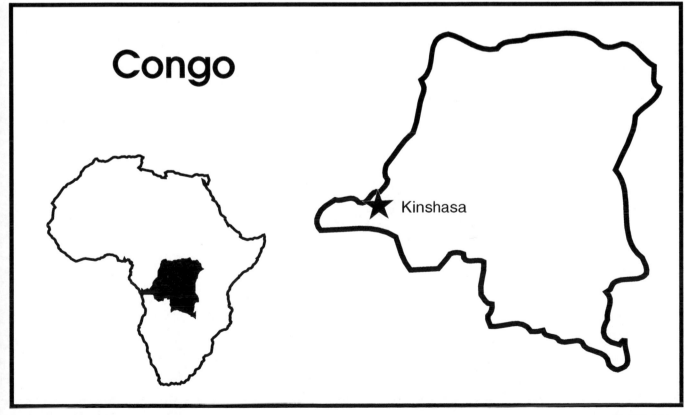

Congo

Kinshasa

Congo Republic

Republic of the Congo

Area in Square Miles: 132,046

Capital: Brazzaville

Climate: tropical rain forest, equatorial

Population in 1997: 2,583,198

Peoples of Congo: Bantu, Kongo, Sangha, M'Boch, Teke, European

Major Languages Spoken in Congo: French, Lingala, Kikongo, others

Religions Practiced in Congo: Christian, traditional indigenous, Muslim

Currency in 1997: 610 CFA francs = $1.00 U.S.

Natural Resources: petroleum, timber, potash, lead, zinc, uranium, copper, natural gas, bauxite

Agriculture: tobacco, coffee, rice, corn, cassava, sugar, peanuts, vegetables, rubber trees, palm oil

Industry: crude oil, cement, sawmills, brewing, sugar mill, palm oil, soap

Interesting Facts: The Congo Republic gained independence from France in 1960. It is rich in natural resources. The rain forests are being cut down to sell as lumber as well as to clear farmland. This land is nutrient poor so the farmers must start over on a newly cleared patch of rain forest. This country is well known for beautiful wooden sculptures. The Congo Republic region has seasonal flooding. This country is the commercial and transport hub of central Africa.

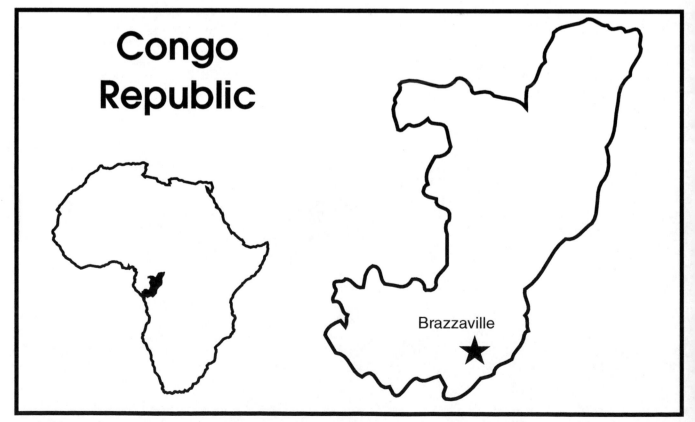

Congo Republic

Brazzaville

Equatorial Guinea

Republic of Equatorial Guinea

Area in Square Miles: 10,820

Capital: Malabo

Climate: tropical, hot, humid

Population in 1997: 442,516

Peoples of Equatorial Guinea: Fang, Bubi, some Spanish

Major Languages Spoken in Equatorial Guinea: Spanish, Fang, Benge, Combe, Bujeba, Bubi

Religions Practiced in Equatorial Guinea: Roman Catholic, traditional indigenous

Currency in 1997: 610 CFA francs = $1.00 U.S.

Natural Resource: wood

Agriculture: cocoa, coffee, timber, rice, yams, bananas

Industry: fishing, sawmilling, palm-oil processing

Interesting Facts: In 1968 Equatorial Guinea gained independence from Spain. Spain remains the main trading partner. Nigeria and Cameroon are other important trading partners. The United States is involved in the production and export of local oil and gas. The soil of Equatorial Guinea is very rich and good for farming. Forests of okoume, mahogany, and walnut grow here.

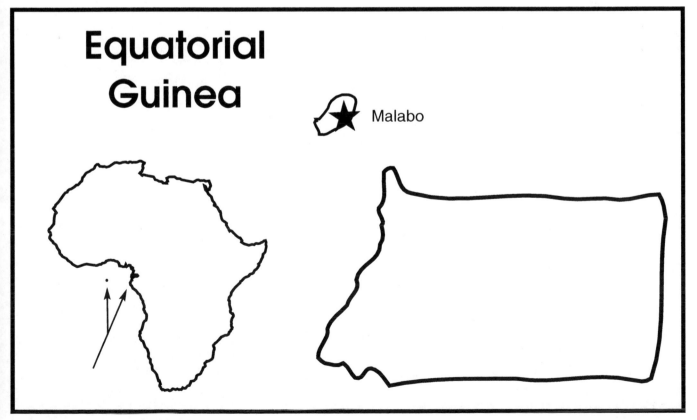

Equatorial Guinea

Malabo

Gabon

Gabonese Republic

Area in Square Miles: 103,346

Capital: Libreville

Climate: coastal, tropical rain forest

Population in 1997: 1,190,159

Peoples of Gabon: Bantu, Fang, Sira, Bapounou, Bateke, Europeans

Major Languages Spoken in Gabon: French, Fang, Myene, Bateke, Bandjabi

Religions Practiced in Gabon: Christian, Muslim, indigenous beliefs

Currency in 1997: 610 CFA francs = $1.00 U.S.

Natural Resources: lumber, rubber, uranium, gold, crude oil, iron ore

Agriculture: cocoa, coffee, wood, palm oil, rice, pineapples, bananas, manioc, peanuts, root crops

Industry: oil production, mineral mining, lumber, textiles

Interesting Facts: Gabon gained independence from the French in 1960. The great rivers of Gabon are the traditional way for travel and trade by boat. These rivers can also be used to produce hydroelectric power. There is plentiful rainfall in Gabon, but 30% of the land is rain forest with poor soil for food crops. Only about 1% of the land is suitable for growing crops; therefore, Gabon must import food to feed the population. Every year rain forest timber is cut for sale and for new croplands.

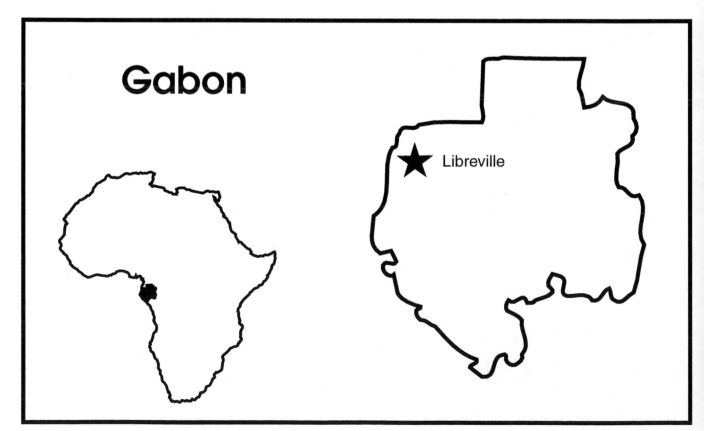

Gabon

Libreville

São Tomé and Príncipe
Democratic Republic of São Tomé and Príncipe

Area in Square Miles: 387

Capital: São Tomé

Climate: tropical

Population in 1997: 147,865

Peoples of São Tomé and Príncipe: Mesticos (Portuguese-African mixture), African

Major Languages Spoken in São Tomé and Príncipe: Portuguese, Fang, Kriolu

Religions Practiced in São Tomé and Príncipe: Roman Catholic, Protestant, traditional indigenous

Currency in 1997: 2,833 dobras = $1.00 U.S.

Natural Resource: fish

Agriculture: cocoa, coconut oil, copra, tourism, manufacturing, construction

Interesting Facts: In 1975 São Tomé and Príncipe gained independence from the Portuguese who first settled the land in the 1500s. Large sugar plantations were once run by the Portuguese using African slaves. Today coffee and cocoa are important exports. Local fishing for tuna is often done in canoes, using traditional style nets. Many tourists now go to this country to fish and sightsee. This country consists of the volcanic islands of São Tomé, Príncipe, Pedras, Rolas, and Tinhosas.

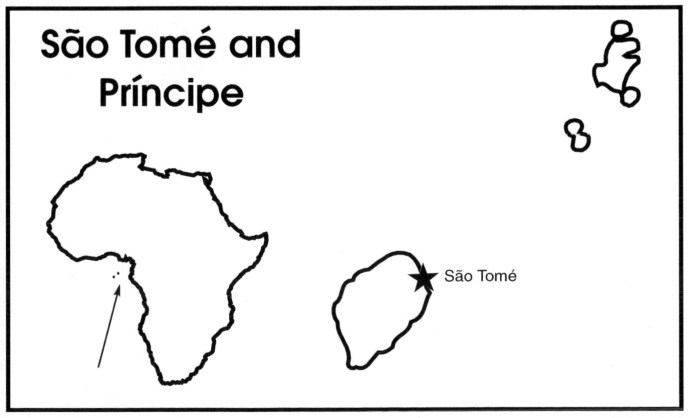

São Tomé and Príncipe

São Tomé

A Visit to Eastern Africa

Mount Kilmanjaro and Mount Kenya, volcanic mountains, rise above the grasslands of eastern Africa. The Great Rift Valley is located in this region. Lake Victoria, one of several large, deep, beautiful lakes of the Great Rift Valley, is the source of the great Nile River. Grasslands stretch down the eastern coast to southern Africa.

Burundi

Republic of Burundi

Area in Square Miles: 10,759

Capital: Bujumbura

Climate: tropical to temperate

Population in 1997: 6,052,614

Peoples of Burundi: Hutu, Tutsi, Twa

Major Languages Spoken in Burundi: Kirundi, French, Swahili

Religions Practiced in Burundi: Roman Catholic, Protestant, traditional indigenous

Currency in 1997: 347.75 Burundi francs = $1.00 U.S.

Natural Resources: nickel, uranium, cobalt, copper, platinum

Agriculture: coffee, tea, cotton, food crops

Industry: consumer goods, beer brewing

Interesting Facts: Burundi gained its independence from the colonial French in 1962. Lake Tanganyika lies along the western border of Burundi. This lake is an important source of fish. Burundi is divided into three groups: the Twa, the Hutu, and the Tutsi. The short Twa people are believed to be one of the earliest cultures in Africa. The Hutu people are mostly farmers. The Tutsi people are divided into clans and often keep cattle which are a status symbol of wealth.

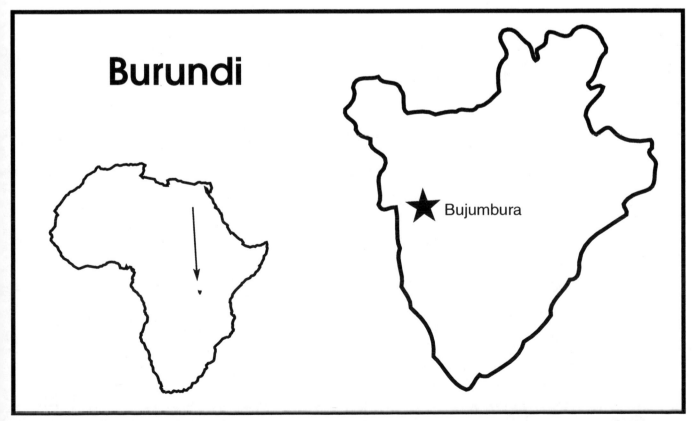

Burundi

Bujumbura

Comoros

Federal Islamic Republic of the Comoros

Area in Square Miles: 838

Capital: Moroni

Climate: tropical, marine

Population in 1997: 589,797

Peoples of Comoros: Arab, African, East Indian

Major Languages Spoken in Comoros: Shaafi-Islam, Swahili, French, Arabic, Comoran

Religions Practiced in Comoros: Muslim, Roman Catholic

Currency in 1997: 452.61 francs = $1.00 U.S.

Natural Resources: agricultural land

Agriculture: perfume essences, copra, coconuts, cloves, vanilla, cinnamon, yams, rice

Industry: perfume distillation, tourism, textiles

Interesting Facts: The Comoran islands were ruled as part of the French colony of Madagascar from 1914 to 1958. Most of the families on these islands fish on the coastal areas or are farmers. Others work to make perfumes from sweet smelling flowers and herbs. During the rainy season (December to April), fierce storms can cause tidal waves in the Comoros islands. Volcanic mountains are found here. Mount Kartala on Grand Comore is an active volcano.

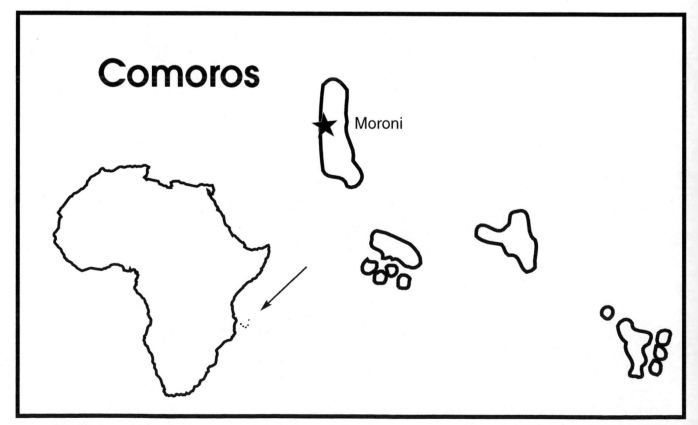

Djibouti

Republic of Djibouti

Area in Square Miles: 8,960

Capital: Djibouti

Climate: arid to semi-arid

Population in 1997: 434,116

Peoples of Djibouti: Somali, Afar

Major Languages Spoken in Djibouti: French, Arabic, Somali, Saho-Afar

Religions Practiced in Djibouti: Muslim, Christian

Currency in 1997: 177 Djibouti francs = $1.00 U.S.

Natural Resources: farmland

Agriculture: goats, sheep, camels, cattle, coffee

Industry: port and maritime support, mineral-water bottling, dairy products

Interesting Facts: The port of Djibouti is important for sea trade across the Red Sea. In 1888 France acquired the port of Djibouti for its own trade purposes. In 1977 Djibouti gained independence. The lack of inland water and fertile land in the rural areas has caused many people to move to the capital city to seek employment. The government is planting trees to hold back the desert sands. Important trading partners include Somalia and Yemen.

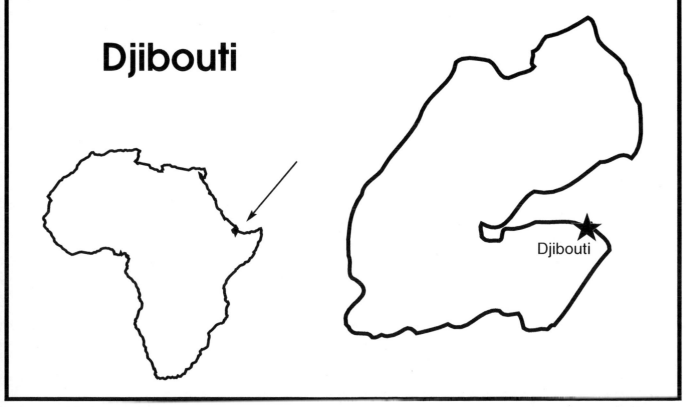

Djibouti

Djibouti

Eritrea
State of Eritrea

Area in Square Miles: 46,829

Capital: Asmara

Climate: hot and dry seacoast area, cool and wet in highlands, cool and wet central highlands

Population in 1997: 3,589,687

Peoples of Eritrea: Afar, Tigre, Tigrinya, Kunama, Saho

Major Languages Spoken in Eritrea: Tigrinya, Amharic, Tigre

Religions Practiced in Eritrea: Muslim, Christian, Protestant

Currency in 1997: 7.2 birrs = $1.00 U.S.

Natural Resources: gold, copper, iron ore, potash

Agriculture: sorghum, livestock, fish, lentils, citrus fruits, vegetables, maize, cotton, tobacco, coffee, sisal

Industry: food processing, beverages, clothing, textiles

Interesting Facts: From 1941 to 1952 Britain occupied Eritrea. Ethiopia annexed Eritrea in 1961, and it became an Ethiopian province. Ethiopia granted independence to Eritrea in 1993. Ethiopia needs the port of Eritrea for trade. The eastern coast of Eritrea lies on the Red Sea. Trade is carried across the Red Sea by ships. The State of Eritrea is now forming a new government. Efforts are being made to improve the economy and educational system to make the country more stable. Water is in short supply in most areas. Some people here are pastoral nomads, but most of the population are farmers or factory workers.

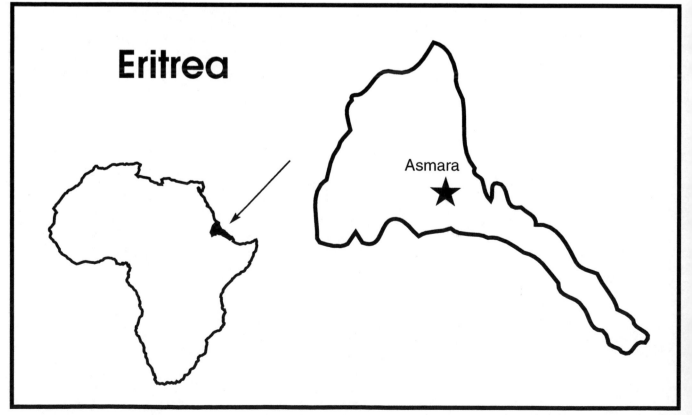

Eritrea

Asmara

Ethiopia

Federal Democratic Republic of Ethiopia

Area in Square Miles: 471,800

Capital: Addis Ababa

Climate: temperate in highlands, arid to semi-arid in lowlands

Population in 1997: 58,732,577

Peoples of Ethiopia: Oromo, Amhara, Tigre, Sidamo, others

Major Languages Spoken in Ethiopia: Amharic, Tigrinya, Oromo, Somali, Arabic, Italian, English

Religions Practiced in Ethiopia: Muslim, Ethiopian-Orthodox, others

Currency in 1997: 6.81 birrs = $1.00 U.S.

Natural Resources: potash, gold, salt, copper, platinum

Agriculture: cereals, coffee, pulse, oilseeds, livestock

Industry: processed food, textiles, cement, building materials, hydroelectric power

Interesting Facts: Ethiopia has never been colonized by Europeans. Great palaces and churches made from stone and carved wood are still standing from early empires. Coptic Christian churches were carved from solid rock over 700 years ago under King Labila. Ethiopia is well known for fine jewelry which is worn as crosses, necklaces, and bracelets. According to tradition, the early kingdom of Theiopia was started by Menelik I, the son of Solomon and Queen of Sheba.

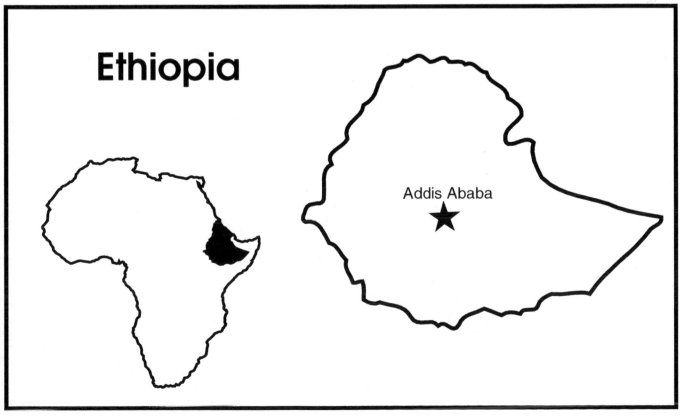

Ethiopia

Addis Ababa

Kenya
Republic of Kenya

Area in Square Miles: 224,900

Capital: Nairobi

Climate: tropical to semi-arid

Population in 1997: 28,803,085

Peoples of Kenya: Turkana, Kikuyu, Luhya, Luo, Kalenjin, Maasai, Kamba

Major Languages Spoken in Kenya: English, Swahili, Kikuyu, Lou, Kamba, Kipsigi, Maasai, Luhya

Religions Practiced in Kenya: traditional indigenous, Protestant, Roman Catholic

Currency in 1997: 69.88 Kenyan shillings = $1.00 U.S.

Natural Resources: wildlife, farmland, soda ash, wattle

Agriculture: corn, wheat, rice, sugarcane, coffee, tea, sisal, livestock, coconuts, cotton

Industry: petroleum products, cement, beer, automobile assembly, food processing, tourism

Interesting Facts: In 1963 Kenya gained independence from the British. Kenya is the commercial center of eastern Africa. Swahili city-states which grew along the eastern coast were built by trade with Asia. The Maasai and Turkana are traditionally nomadic cattle herders. They exchange cattle for food crops grown by the Kamba, Luo, Kikuyu and others. Kenya has large wildlife parks that are popular with tourists. Tsavo National Park is here. Kenya may be the home of the first humans on Earth according to fossil records.

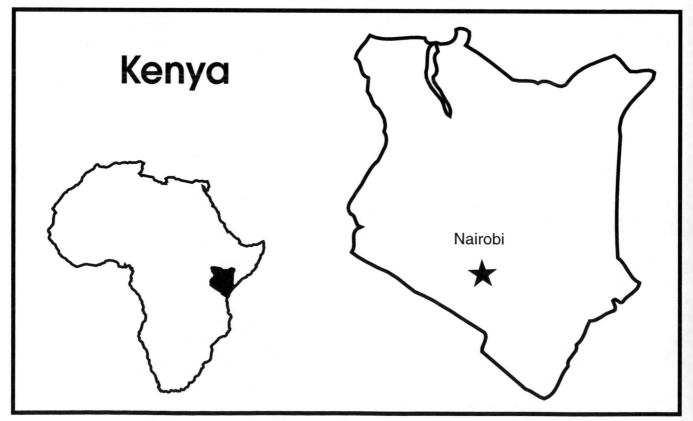

Kenya

Nairobi ★

Madagascar
Republic of Madagascar

Area in Square Miles: 226,658

Capital: Antananarivo

Climate: tropical, moderate, marine

Population in 1997: 14,061,627

Peoples of Madagascar: Malayo-Indonesian, Cotiers, French, Indian, Creole, Comoran

Major Languages Spoken in Madagascar: Malagasy, French

Religions Practiced in Madagascar: traditional indigenous, Christian, Muslim

Currency in 1997: 5,426.92 Malagasy francs = $1.00 U.S.

Natural Resources: graphites, chrome, coal, bauxite, ilmenite, tar sands, semiprecious stones, timber, mica, nickel

Agriculture: rice, livestock, coffee, vanilla, sugar, cloves, cotton, sisal, peanuts, tobacco

Industry: food processing, textiles, mining, paper, petroleum refining, automobile assembly, construction, cement, farming

Interesting Facts: In 1960, Madagascar gained independence from the French. Because this island has been isolated from the mainland of Africa for so long, there are many plants and animals that can only be found here. The now extinct dodo bird once lived in the tropical forest here. The government now protects endangered species. Peoples from many lands have come by boat to Madagascar and settled on this beautiful island in the Indian Ocean.

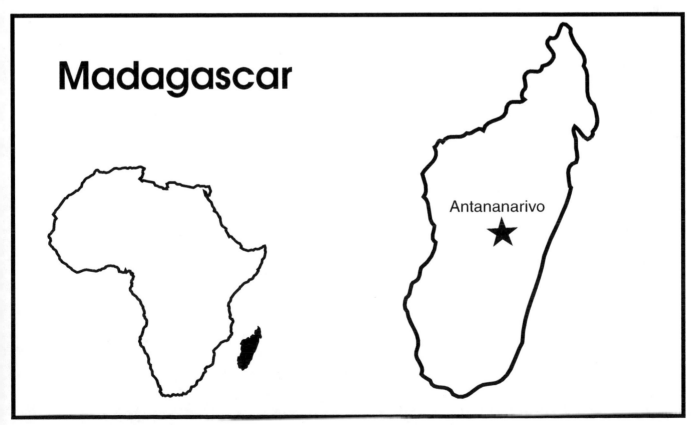

Madagascar

Antananarivo

Mauritius

Republic of Mauritius

Area in Square Miles: 720

Capital: Port Louis

Climate: subtropical, marine

Population in 1997: 1,154,272

Peoples of Mauritius: Indo-Mauritian, Creole, others

Major Languages Spoken in Mauritius: English, French, Creole, Hinki, Urdu

Religions Practiced in Mauritius: Hindu, Christian, Muslim, other

Currency in 1997: 21.65 rupees = $1.00 U.S.

Natural Resources: farmland, fish

Agriculture: sugar, tea, tobacco, corn, potatoes, bananas, cattle, goats, chickens

Industry: sugar production, consumer goods, goods for export, tourism

Interesting Facts: Mauritius gained independence from the British in 1968. This island lies in the Indian Ocean. Farming, fishing, and foreign trade are important for the economy. Mountains encircle the central plateau of this island. Mauritius is developing their economy through tourism. Visitors enjoy the natural beauty of the land. About 90% of the cultivated farm land is used to grow sugarcane, which is a major export item. The islands of Mauritius are surrounded by coral reefs.

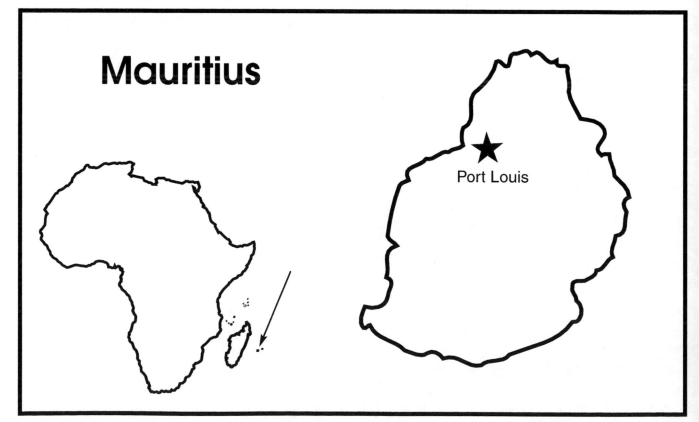

Mauritius

Port Louis

Rwanda

Republic of Rwanda

Area in Square Miles: 10,169

Capital: Kigali

Climate: temperate

Population in 1997: 7,737,537

Peoples of Rwanda: Hutu, Tutsi, Twa

Major Languages Spoken in Rwanda: Kinyarwanda, French, Swahili

Religions Practiced in Rwanda: Christian, traditional indigenous, Muslim

Currency in 1997: 295.50 francs = $1.00 U.S.

Natural Resources: tungsten, tin, cassiterite, natural gas, hydropower

Agriculture: coffee, tea, pyrethrum, beans, potatoes, rice, cassava, plantains

Industry: food processing, mining, consumer goods

Interesting Facts: Rwanda gained independence in 1962 from the French. The Kivu Lake lies along the west coast of Rwanda. Rwanda has seasonal droughts. The weather is cool and wet in the Virunga Mountains which lie on the northwest border between Rwanda and the Congo. Recent civil unrest has upset the lives of the people of Rwanda, sending many to seek refuge in neighboring countries. Most of the population of Rwanda are farmers.

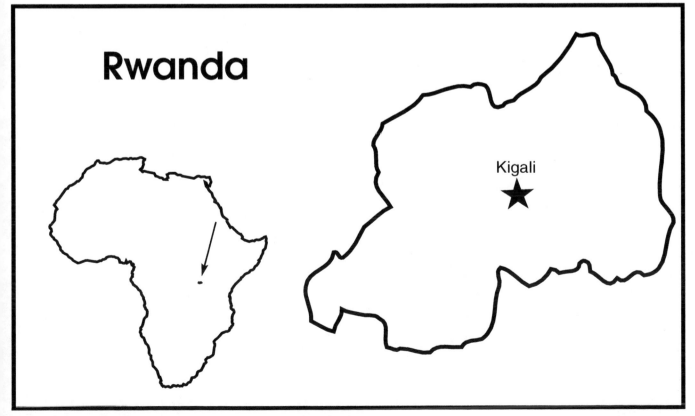

Rwanda

Kigali

Seychelles
Republic of Syechelles

Area in Square Miles: 175

Capital: Victoria

Climate: subtropical, marine

Population in 1997: 78,142

Peoples of Seychelles: Seychellois (mixture of Asians, Africans, and French)

Major Languages Spoken in Seychelles: English, French, Creole

Religions Practiced in Seychelles: Roman Catholic, Anglican, other

Currency in 1997: 5.10 rupees = $1.00 U.S.

Natural Resources: farmland, fish

Agriculture: vanilla, coconuts, cinnamon

Industry: tourism, copra and vanilla processing, coconut oil, construction

Interesting Facts: In 1976 the Seychelles gained independence from England. The Seychelles are a group of small islands and the smallest country in Africa. The coco de mer ("sea coconut") palm tree comes from the Seychelles. The Seychelles is a world leader in wildlife preservation and has large wildlife refuge areas. The 85 islands that make up the Seychelles are in the Indian Ocean.

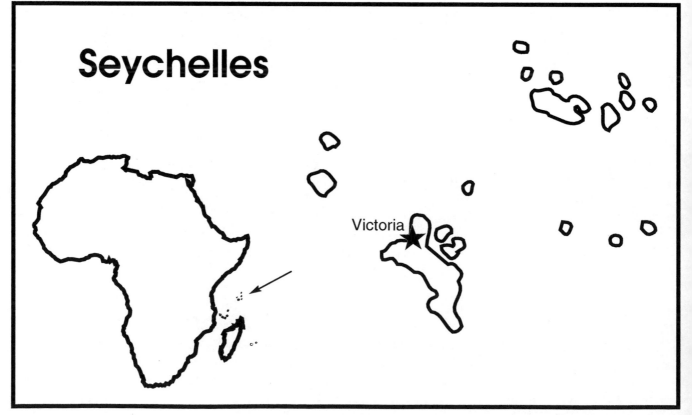

Somalia

Somali Democratic Republic

Area in Square Miles: 246,331

Capital: Mogadishu

Climate: arid to semi-arid

Population in 1997: 9,940,232

Peoples of Somalia: Somali

Major Languages Spoken in Somalia:
Somali, Arabic, Oromo, Italian, English

Religions Practiced in Somalia: Sunni
Muslim, others

Currency in 1997: 4,000 Somali shillings =
$1.00 U.S.

Natural Resources: uranium, timber, fish,
petroleum

Agriculture: livestock, bananas, sugarcane,
cotton, cereals, maize

Industry: sugar refining, tuna and beef
canning, textiles, iron-rod plants, petroleum
refining

Interesting Facts: Somalia lies on the "Horn
of Africa," which resembles a cow horn. In
1960 Somalia gained independence from the
British and Italians, who jointly ruled the area
for 75 years. Traditionally the people of
Somalia were farmers and nomadic herders
of goats, sheep, camels, and cattle. Many
animals were sold in Saudi Arabia, across the
Indian Ocean. Locusts and drought are
common in Somalia.

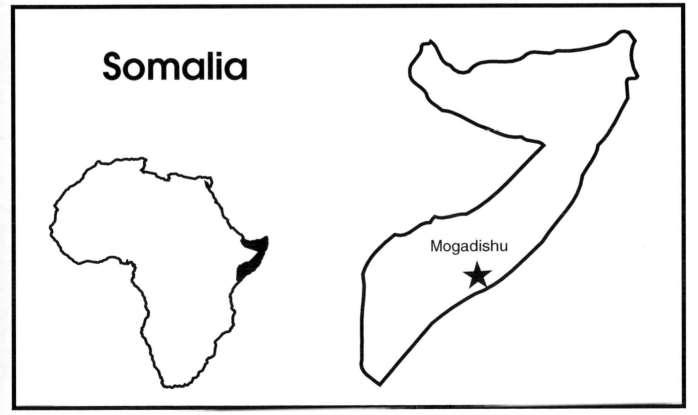

Somalia

Mogadishu

Sudan

Republic of the Sudan

Area in Squares Miles: 967,500

Capital: Khartoum

Climate: desert in north to tropical in south

Population in 1997: 32,594,128

Peoples of Sudan: African, Arab, Beja, others

Major Languages Spoken in Sudan: Arabic, Nuer, Dinka, Shilluki, Masalatis, Fur, Nubian, English, others

Religions Practiced in Sudan: Sunni Muslim, traditional indigenous, Christian

Currency in 1997: 1,615 Sudanese pounds = $1.00 U.S.

Natural Resources: oil, iron ore, copper, chrome

Agriculture: cotton, peanuts, sesame, gum arabic, sorghum, wheat

Industry: textiles, cement, cotton ginning, edible oils, brewing, medicines

Interesting Facts: In 1956 Sudan gained independence from Britain. The port cities on the Red Sea have been trade centers for Sudan for thousands of years. The ancient empire of Nubia once stood on the land that is now called Sudan. The arts and culture of Nubia were similar to the culture of the Egyptian Pharaohs. Queen Tye, the mother of the Egyptian Pharaoh Akhneton, was from Nubia. Sudan is divided into six regions.

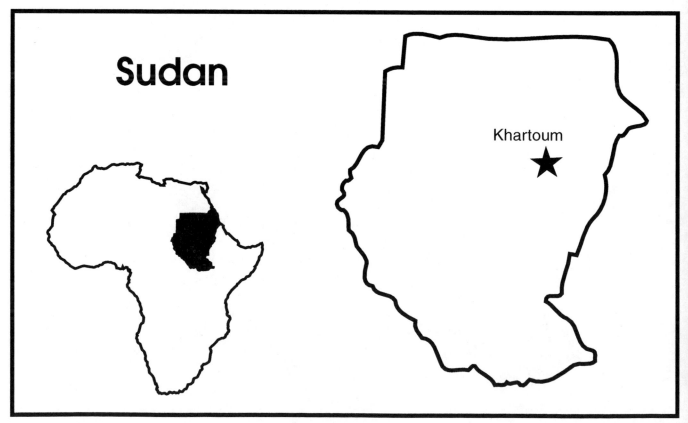

Sudan

Khartoum

Tanzania

United Republic of Tanzania

Area in Square Miles: 364,900

Capital: Dar-es-Salaam

Climate: tropical coast, temperate highlands

Population in 1997: 29,460,753

Peoples of Tanzania: over 100 indigenous groups, Asian, European, Arabic

Major Languages Spoken in Tanzania: Swahili, English, many indigenous dialects

Religions Practiced in Tanzania: Christian, Muslim, indigenous beliefs

Currency in 1997: 629.50 Tanzanian shillings = $1.00 U.S.

Natural Resources: tin, iron ore, coal, diamonds, gemstones, gold, natural gas, nickel, phosphates

Agriculture: coffee, cashews, cloves, tea, cotton, tobacco, wheat, corn, fruits, vegetables, cattle, sheep, goats

Industry: agricultural processing, diamond and gold mining, oil refining, textiles, cement, shoes, wood products, fertilizer

Interesting Facts: Tanzania gained independence from Britain in 1961. Tanzania lies on the Indian Ocean between Kenya and Mozambique. The country of Tanzania includes the islands of Pemba, Mafia, and Zanzibar. Lake Victoria, Lake Nyasa, and Lake Tanganika provide plentiful water for crops, travel by boat, and hydroelectric power. Tourists enjoy visiting Victoria Falls, one of the largest waterfalls in the world. Tanzania grows many different foods, but only 5% of the land is suitable for farming. Trading partners include Germany, Japan, Kenya, Hong Kong, America, and the Netherlands.

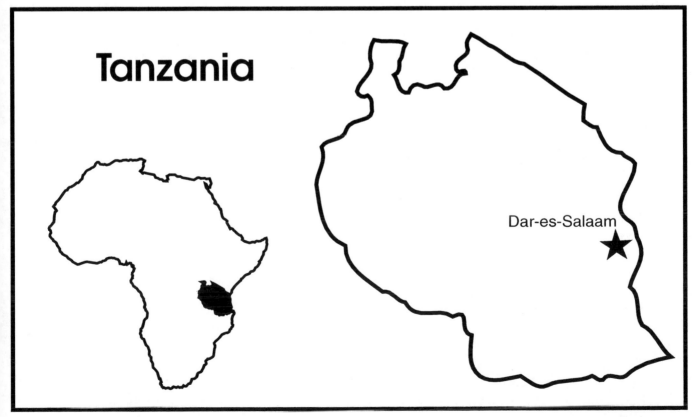

Tanzania

Dar-es-Salaam

Uganda
Republic of Uganda

Area in Square Miles: 91,133

Capital: Kampala

Climate: tropical to semi-arid

Population in 1997: 20,604,874

Peoples of Uganda: Baganda, Karamojong, Basogo, Iteso, Langi, Rwanda, others

Major Languages Spoken in Uganda: English, Luganda, Swahili, Bantu languages, Nilotic languages

Religions Practiced in Uganda: Christian, Muslim, indigenous beliefs

Currency in 1997: 1,110 Ugandan shillings = $1.00 U.S.

Natural Resources: copper, cobalt

Agriculture: coffee, tea, cotton, tobacco, cassava, potatoes, corn, millet, pulse, beef, goats, poultry

Industry: sugar, brewing, tobacco, cotton textiles, cement

Interesting Facts: Uganda gained independence from Britain in 1962. Due to fertile soil and ample rainfall, Uganda is self-sufficient in food production. There are many farmers in Uganda. Coffee is the major crop and is exported to many countries, including France, Britain, Spain, and America. The Cheewezi are legendary rulers of an early kingdom in Uganda. Uganda is known for beautiful textiles.

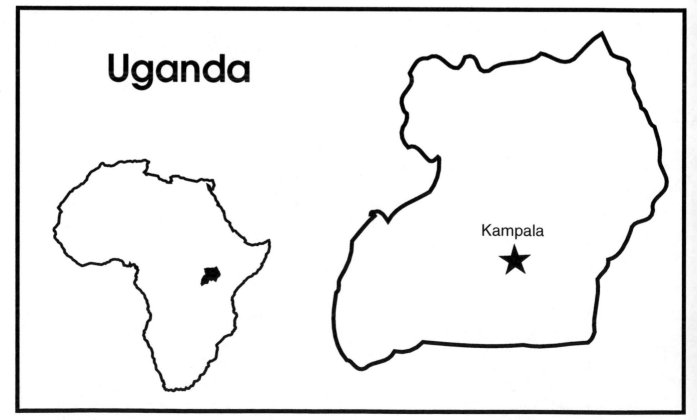

Uganda

Kampala

A Visit to Southern Africa

Mountains, plateaus, and rolling hills are characteristic of southern Africa. The Kalahari Desert lies in southern Africa. Much of the land is used for subsistence farming and grazing. Part of the High Africa land region, southern Africa also has deserts, swamps, and forests. The average rainfall in this region ranges 2–60 inches (5–152 cm). The climate varies from tropical wet and dry in the upper part of the region to desert conditions in the lower coastal areas.

Angola

Republic of Angola

Area in Square Miles: 481,354

Capital: Luanda

Climate: tropical

Population in 1997: 10,623,994

Peoples of Angola: Ovimbundu, Mbundu, Kongo, Ngangela, Lunda, others

Major Languages Spoken in Angola: Portuguese, Bantu, native African dialects

Religions Practiced in Angola: Roman Catholic, Protestant, indigenous beliefs

Currency in 1997: 265,000 kwanzas = $1.00 U.S.

Natural Resources: iron, diamonds, gold, oil, phosphates

Agriculture: coffee, sugarcane, bananas

Industry: food processing, textiles, mining, brewing, oil

Interesting Facts: Angola is second only to Nigeria in oil production in southern Africa. It was converted to Christianity by the Portuguese in the 1480s. Portugal established a colonial stronghold in Angola throughout the 1800s. By the 1920s Angola was completely under Portuguese control after the indigenous kingdoms were dismantled. After a civil war, Angola gained independence in 1975. Despite its independence from external influences, internal strife and political instability still prevail today.

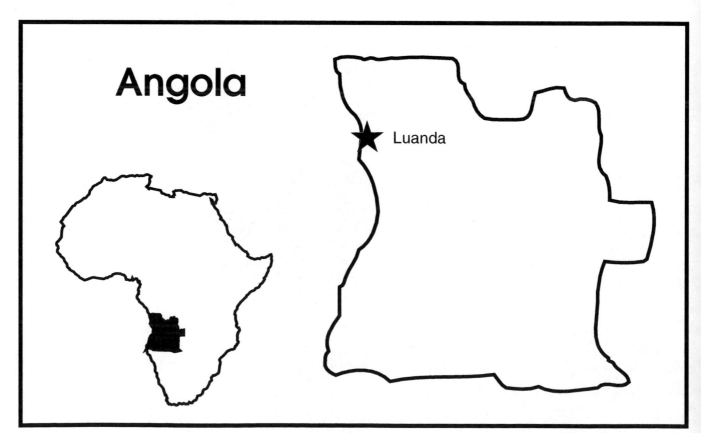

Botswana

Republic of Botswana

Area in Square Miles: 231,804

Capital: Gaborone

Climate: arid, semitropical

Population in 1997: 1,500,765

Peoples of Botswana: Batswana, Kalanga, Basarwa, Kgalagadi, Khiosan, European

Major Languages Spoken in Botswana: English, Setswana

Religions Practiced in Botswana: indigenous beliefs, Christian

Currency in 1997: 3.7 pulas = $1.00 U.S.

Natural Resources: diamonds, copper, nickel, salt, soda ash, potash, coal, gold, silver, natural gas, iron ore, coal

Agriculture: corn, sorghum, millet, cowpeas, livestock such as cattle is raised for exportation

Industry: tourism, livestock processing, diamond mining, copper, nickel, and coal mining

Interesting Facts: Botswana gained independence from the British in 1966. Botswana has great mineral wealth; however, this wealth is not distributed evenly among the population. The Khiosan ("Bushmen") are the earliest inhabitants of this country and perhaps of the entire continent of Africa. They create beautiful paintings called Kuru. Their language consists of "clicking" sounds. The Tswana people migrated into the area about 200 years ago. The Okavango Swamp lies in the northwestern region. This country consists mostly of arid plateaus of rolling hills.

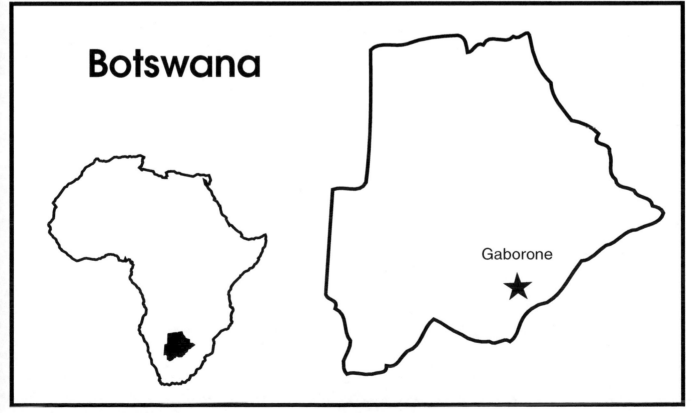

Botswana

Gaborone

Lesotho

Kingdom of Lesotho

Area in Square Miles: 11,720

Capital: Maseru

Climate: semi-arid

Population in 1997: 2,007,814

Peoples of Lesotho: Over 99% of the population are Sotho; the remaining population are Europeans and Asians.

Major Languages Spoken in Lesotho: Sesotho, English, Zulu, Xhosa

Religions Practiced in Lesotho: indigenous beliefs, Christian

Currency in 1997: 4.34 loti = $1.00 U.S.

Natural Resources: diamonds, other minerals, water, farmland, grazing land

Agriculture: livestock, corn, wheat, pulse, sorghum, barley

Industry: tourism, mineral mining, food processing, clothing, textiles

Interesting Facts: Lesotho gained independence from the British in 1966. The Xhosa people are famous for their colorful beadwork. The Zulu people still recall their legendary warrior prince Shaka, who fought to make the British leave southern Africa. This country has abundant water and farmland. This allows for the export of wool, mohair, wheat, cattle, corn, peas, beans, and beautiful woven baskets. Animal hides are also exported. This country is known for the high quality of its schools. Girls are encouraged to study for professional careers.

Malawi

Republic of Malawi

Area in Square Miles: 45,200

Capital: Lilongwe

Climate: temperate

Population in 1997: 9,609,081

Peoples of Malawi: Chewa, Nyanga, Tumbuko, Lomwe, Ngonde, Ngoni, Tonga, Senaa

Major Languages Spoken in Malawi: English, Chichewa, others

Religions Practiced in Malawi: Protestant, Muslim, Roman Catholic

Currency in 1997: 17.36 kwachas = $1.00 U.S.

Natural Resources: limestone, uranium, coal, bauxite

Agriculture: sugar, tea, coffee, peanuts, cotton, corn, sorghum, millet, root crops

Industry: food processing

Interesting Facts: Malawi gained independence from the British in 1964. Malawi is one of the few countries in Africa that has sufficient rainfall without droughts. Malawi does not need to import food to feed the population. About one-fourth of the country is farmland. About one-third of the country is covered with forests. The Great Rift Valley is an outstanding natural feature of Malawi. The remaining land is pastures and meadows. Lake Malawi covers about one-fifth of the country area. The 15th century Malawi Kingdom is famous in legend. Malawi was once called Nyasaland.

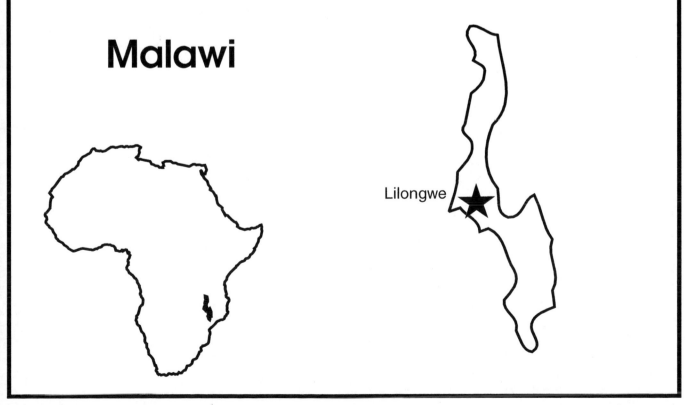

Malawi

Lilongwe

Mozambique

Republic of Mozambique

Areas in Square Miles: 302,328

Capital: Maputo

Climate: semi-arid, temperate ocean coast

Population in 1997: 18,165,476

Peoples of Mozambique: indigenous groups, Europeans, Euro-Africans, Indians

Major Languages Spoken in Mozambique: many indigenous dialects, Portuguese

Religions Practiced in Mozambique: indigenous beliefs, Christian, Muslim

Currency in 1997: 11,300 meticals = $1.00 U.S.

Natural Resources: coal, titanium, gold

Agriculture: sugar, copra, citrus fruits, sisal, cassava, roots and tubers, cashews, fishing, tobacco

Industry: beverages, glass, asbestos, fertilizer, soap, paints, petroleum products, textiles, cement, tourism

Interesting Facts: Mozambique gained independence from the Portuguese in 1975. Most of the population farms the small areas of fertile land. Over half of the country is meadow and pasture. About 20% of the land is covered with forests. There are many rivers in this country. The great Zambezi River travels 290 miles across Mozambique. The rivers are used for trade and travel by boat. This country has cool winters and hot tropical summers. Mt. Binga is the tallest mountain in Mozambique.

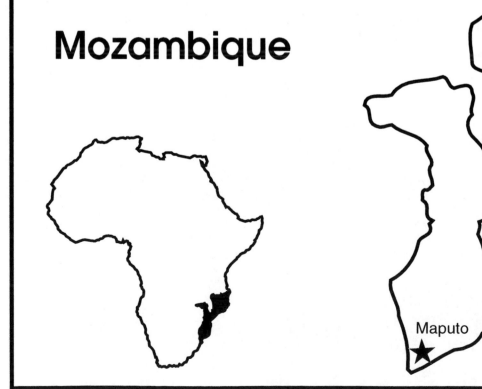

Mozambique

Maputo

Namibia

Republic of Namibia

Area in Square Miles: 318,000

Capital: Windhoek

Climate: arid, temperate

Population in 1997: 1,727,183

Peoples of Namibia: Ovambo, other African groups, European

Major Languages Spoken in Namibia: Afrikaans, German, English, other indigenous dialects

Religions Practiced in Namibia: Christian, indigenous beliefs

Currency in 1997: 4.69 Namibian dollars = $1.00 U.S.

Natural Resources: mineral wealth, gold, diamonds, uranium, silver, tin, copper, lithium

Agriculture: beef, sheep, goats, millet, sorghum, corn, wheat

Industry: gold and other mineral mining and processing

Interesting Facts: Namibia gained independence from South Africa in 1990. Namibia was a German colony from 1884 to 1917. This country is not heavily populated. The northern areas have good rainfall, but the south has droughts. The western edge of the Kalahari Desert extends into Namibia. The Namib Desert lies along the Atlantic coast. Gold and diamonds brought European missionaries, traders, and settlers to Namibia. Apartheid divided the European settlers from the African population for many years. Most of the mineral wealth was kept by the European minority. Now there is an effort to redistribute the wealth.

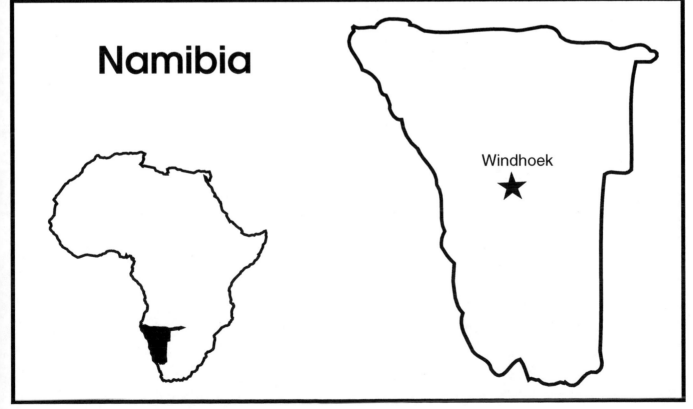

Namibia

Windhoek ★

South Africa

Republic of South Africa

Area in Square Miles: 437,872

Capital: Cape Town (legislative), Pretoria (executive), Bloemfontein (judicial)

Climate: temperate, semi-arid

Population in 1997: 42,427,458

Peoples of South Africa: numerous African groups, Europeans

Major Languages Spoken in South Africa: Afrikaans, English, Ndebele, Pedi, Sotho, Swati, Tsonga, Tswana, Venda, Xhosa, Zulu

Religions Practiced in South Africa: Christian, Hindu, Muslim

Currency in 1997: 4.69 rands = $1.00 U.S.

Natural Resources: gold, diamonds, mineral ores, uranium, fish

Agriculture: corn, wool, wheat, sugarcane, tobacco, citrus fruits, dairy products

Industry: mining, automobile assembly, metal working, machinery, textiles, iron and steel, fertilizer, fishing, chemicals

Interesting Facts: In 1994, South Africa gained freedom from the system of apartheid (separatehood). Nobel Peace Prize winner Nelson Mandela is the president. In 1652 Dutch settlers went to South Africa and traded and farmed. In 1830 the British took control. Independence from the British was gained in 1910. The Zulu prince Shaka led battles against the British. As a young man, Mahatma Gandhi also worked in South Africa against the British rulers. Archbishop Desmond Tutu was awarded a Nobel Peace Prize for his nonviolent protest against apartheid. Apartheid kept all of the natural wealth of South Africa in the hands of the European minority. A rich country, South Africa is now rebuilding school programs and businesses to include Africans.

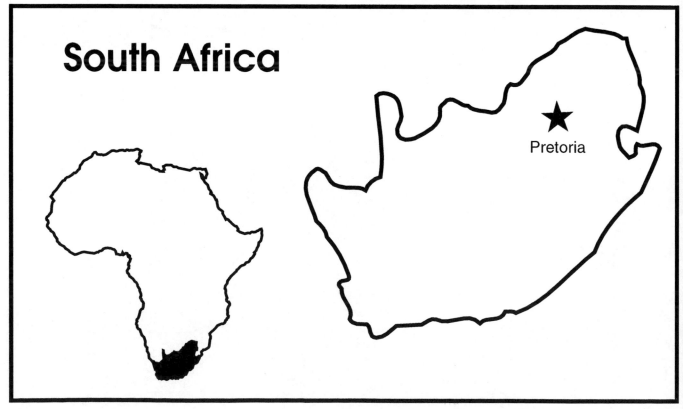

South Africa

Pretoria

Swaziland

Kingdom of Swaziland

Area in Square Miles: 6,705

Capital: Mbabane

Climate: semi-arid, temperate

Population in 1997: 1,031,600

Peoples of Swaziland: Over 95% African, 3% European

Major Languages Spoken in Swaziland: English, siSwati (Zulu dialect)

Religions Practiced in Swaziland: indigenous beliefs, Christian

Currency in 1997: 4.69 lilangenis = $1.00 U.S.

Natural Resources: coal, clay, asbestos, diamonds, gold, forests, hydroelectric power

Agriculture: maize, cotton, rice, sugar, citrus fruits, tobacco

Industry: mining coal and asbestos, wood pulp, sugar processing, canned fruits

Interesting Facts: Swaziland became a British colony in 1903 and gained independence from the British in 1968. Swaziland is covered by the Le Bombo mountains, forests, and plateaus. Four major river systems are found in Swaziland. These large rivers provide hydroelectric power to the population in the cities and countryside. Swaziland trades with South Africa, the United Kingdom and the United States. Most of the population are farmers.

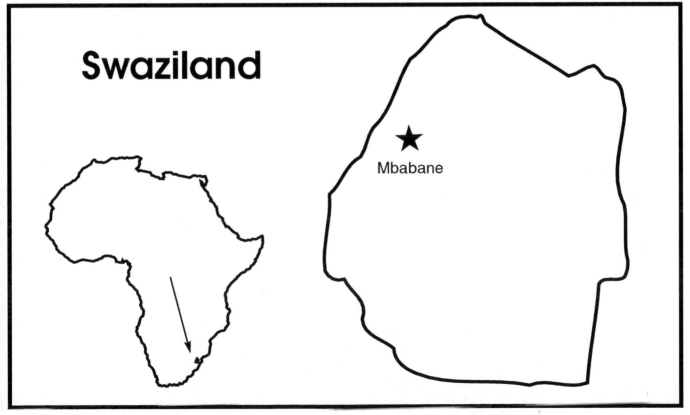

Swaziland

Mbabane

Zambia

Republic of Zambia

Area in Square Miles: 290,584

Capital: Lusaka

Climate: temperate, semitropical

Population in 1997: 9,349,975

Peoples of Zambia: Shona, Ndebele, European, Asian, Ila-Tonga, Bemba

Major Languages Spoken in Zambia: English, Shona, Ndebele

Religions Practiced in Zambia: Christian, Muslim, Hindu, indigenous beliefs

Currency in 1997: 1,323 kwachas = $1.00 U.S.

Natural Resources: copper, cobalt, zinc, lead, coal, emeralds, gold, silver, uranium

Agriculture: tobacco, corn, cotton, fruits, groundnuts

Industry: copper mining and processing, construction, foodstuffs, chemicals, beverages, textiles, fertilizers

Interesting Facts: In 1964 Zambia gained independence from the British who colonized Zambia in 1890. This country is well known for its colorful printed textiles. The Ndebele homes are often painted both indoors and outdoors with bright colors in geometrical patterns by the women. Zambia is a wealthy country and has precious forest reserves as well as large rivers. The magnificent Victoria Falls and Lake Kariba lie on the border of Zambia and Zimbabwe. Each year many tourists go on photo safaris to Zambia's wildlife parks.

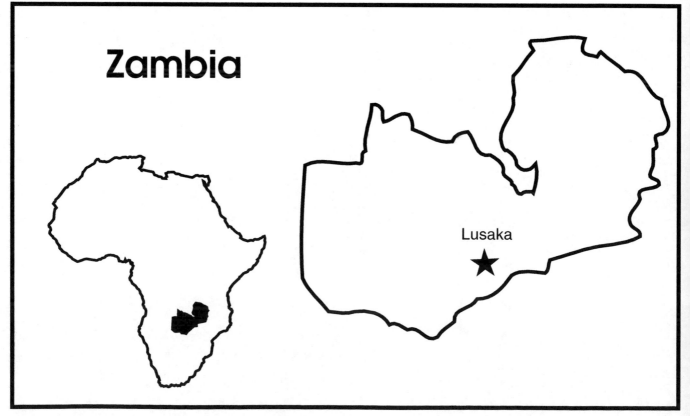

Zimbabwe

Republic of Zimbabwe

Area in Square Miles: 150,803

Capital: Harare

Climate: temperate

Population in 1997: 11,423,175

Peoples of Zimbabwe: Shona, Ndebele, other African groups, 1% European, 1% Asian

Major Languages Spoken in Zimbabwe: English, Shona, Ndebele

Religions Practiced in Zimbabwe: traditional indigenous, Syncretic (Christian-indigenous mix)

Currency in 1997: 11.60 Zimbabwe dollars = $1.00 U.S.

Natural Resources: coal, asbestos, gold, nickel, copper, iron, tin, lithium, chromium ore, vanadium

Agriculture: grains, wheat, cereals, cotton, corn, tobacco, tea, sugar, livestock

Industry: mineral mining, processing, clothing, chemicals

Interesting Facts: Zimbabwe gained independence from the British in 1980. Zimbabwe has spectacular natural features such as Victoria Falls, Mt. Inyangani, and Lake Kariba. The 11th century Empire of Zimbabwe left a legacy of beautiful, tall stone buildings that still stand in the southeast of the country. Hardwood forests are found in the southeast. Iron-age cultures were replaced by migrating Bantu speaking groups in the fifth century.

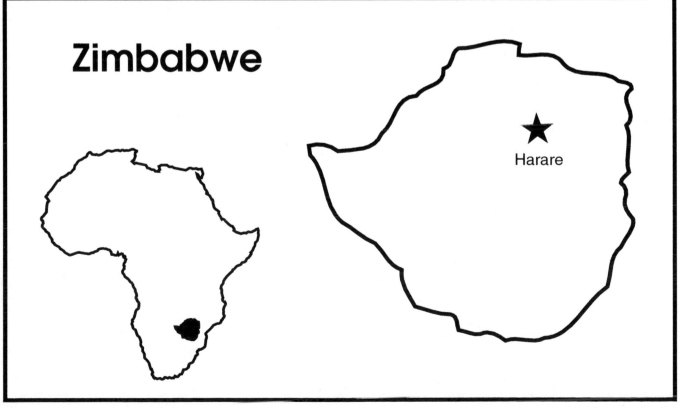

Zimbabwe

Harare

Labelled Political Map of Africa

North Atlantic Ocean

Black Sea

Caspian Sea

Mediterranean Sea

MOROCCO

TUNISIA

Canary Islands (SPAIN)

ALGERIA

LIBYA

EGYPT

WESTERN SAHARA

CAPE VERDE

MAURITANIA

MALI

NIGER

Red Sea

ERITREA

SENEGAL

THE GAMBIA

CHAD

Lake Chad

SUDAN

DJIBOUTI

BURKINA

GUINEA

GUINEA BISSAU

BENIN

SIERRA LEONE

CÔTE D'IVOIRE

GHANA

NIGERIA

SOMALIA

CENTRAL AFRICAN REPUBLIC

ETHIOPIA

Indian Ocean

TOGO

CAMEROON

Lake Turkana

LIBERIA

SÃO TOMÉ & PRÍNCIPE

Lake Albert

UGANDA

KENYA

Lake Victoria

EQUATORIAL GUINEA

GABON

CONGO REPUBLIC

CONGO

RWANDA

BURUNDI

SEYCHELLES

ANGOLA

TANZANIA

South Atlantic Ocean

Lake Tanganyika

COMOROS

MALAWI

Lake Nyasa

ANGOLA

ZAMBIA

Lake Kariba

MOZAMBIQUE

NAMIBIA

ZIMBABWE

BOTSWANA

MADAGASCAR

MAURITIUS

SOUTH AFRICA (Walvis Bay)

SWAZILAND

SOUTH AFRICA

LESOTHO

1000 Km

1000 Mi.

Blank Political Map of Africa

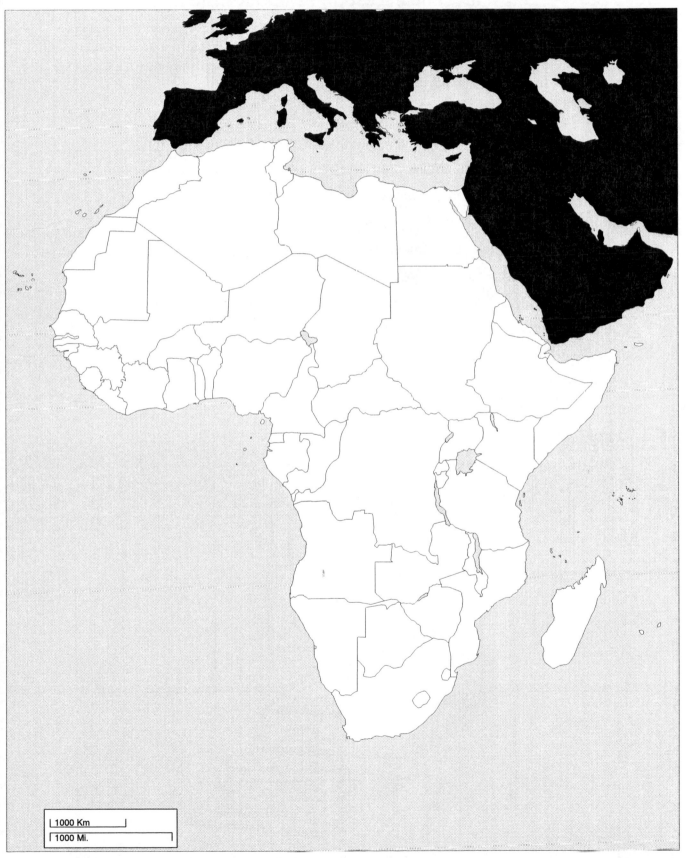

1000 Km

1000 Mi.

World Wide Web Directory

Educational Resources about Africa

The World Wide Web and the Internet have resources that may be useful for individual and class research. This is a directory of selected sites about Africa. Sites on the Internet are constantly changing, and new ones are added daily. Use a Web browser and keywords about Africa or a specific country or topic to discover new links to add to this list.

<http://www.learner.org/content/ed/catalog/edworldcult/edafpage.html>

<http://www.yahooligans.com/Around the World/Cultures/African American/>

<http://www.insead.fr/Encyclopedia/Economics/Religions/Africa/>

<http://www.sas.upenn.edu/African Studies/Home Page/AFR GIDE.html>

<http://www.sas.upenn.edu/African Studies/About African/ww k12.html>

<http://www.vtourist.com/webmap/africa.htm>

<http://www.yale.edu/swahili/afrilink.html>

<http://www. Nationalgeographic.com>

<http://www.netnoir.com/index.html>

<http://www.til.org/kt/kente.html>

<http://www.ccph.com>

<http://www.artsmis.org/mythology>

<http://www.lam.mus.ca.us/africa/tour/desert>

World Map

Directions: Find and label the continents and oceans on the map. Color the continent of Africa.

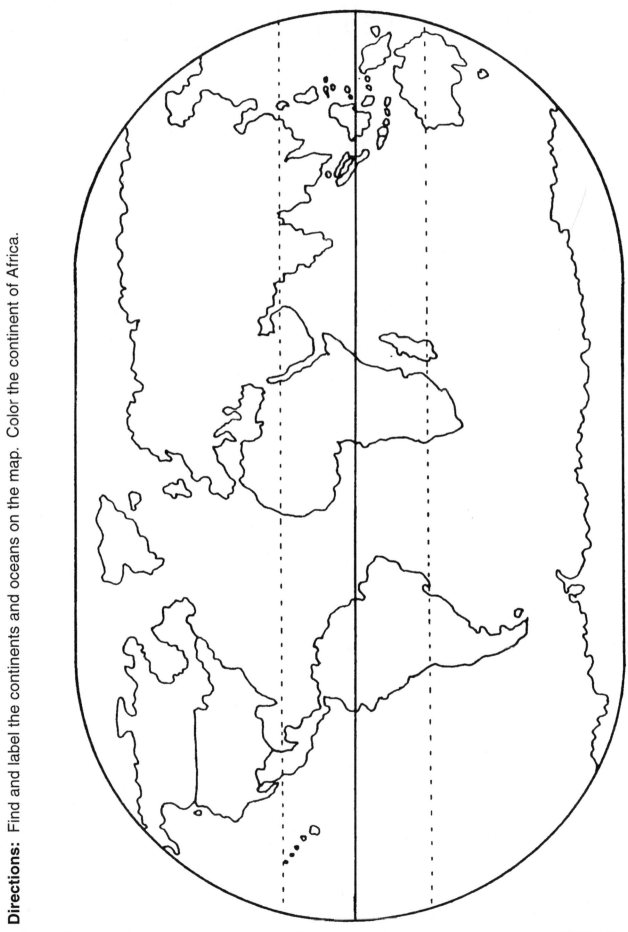

Africa Is Big!

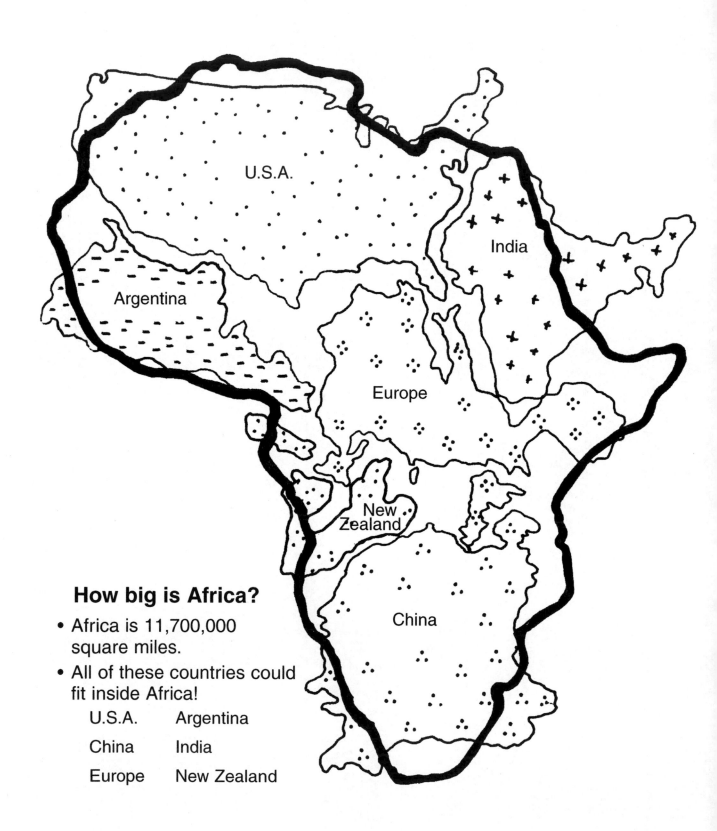

U.S.A.

India

Argentina

Europe

New Zealand

China

How big is Africa?

- Africa is 11,700,000 square miles.
- All of these countries could fit inside Africa!

U.S.A.	Argentina
China	India
Europe	New Zealand

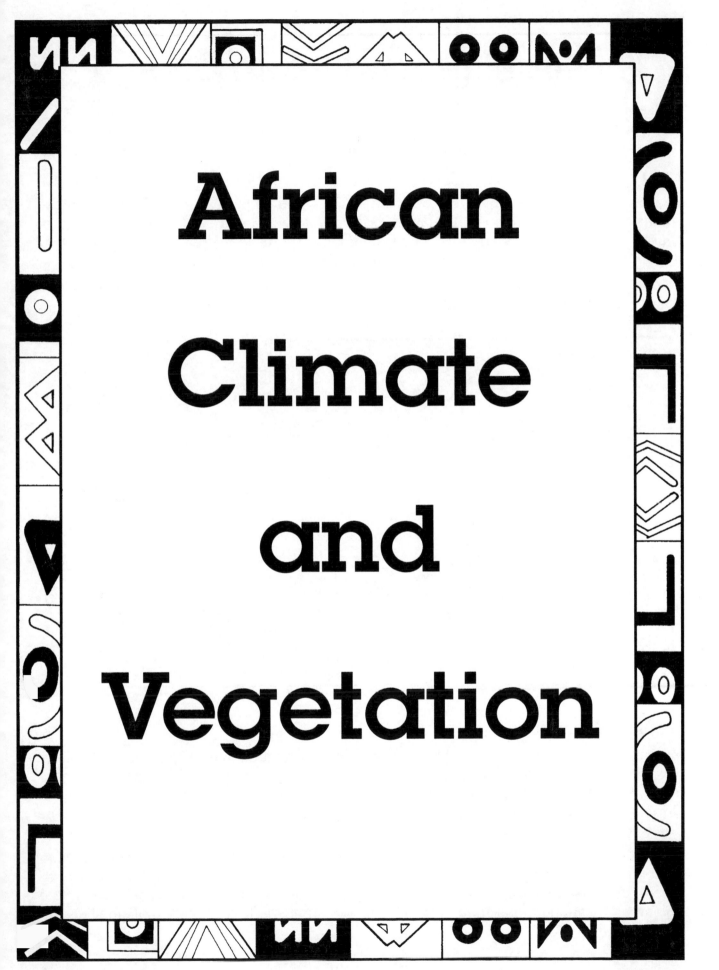

African Climate and Vegetation

Background Information

Unlike the other continents, Africa has a fairly uniform climate. The position of Africa in the Tropical Zone, the lack of mountain chains to serve as climatic barriers, and the force of cool ocean currents contribute to creating this climate.

Rain Forests

The climate in the center of Africa, near the equator, and on the eastern coast of Madagascar is that of a tropical rain forest. The average temperature is about 80° F (26.7° C), and the average annual rainfall is about 70 inches (178 cm). The Guinea coast has a similar climate. Although most of the rain falls in one season on the Guinea coast, no months are rainless.

Vegetation in tropical rain forest zones is dense. Shrubs, ferns, and mosses cover the ground. Evergreens, oil palms, and a variety of tropical hardwood trees tower over the landscape.

Tropical Savannah

Immediately north and south of the rain forest, the climate becomes a tropical savanna, with a wet season during the summer months and a dry season during the winter months. The amount of rain varies from 20 inches (55 cm) to more than 60 inches (152 cm) annually. North of the equator summer comes in July, while south of the equator summer is in January. The tropical savanna climate covers about one-fifth of the African continent.

Vegetation in the savannas varies with the amount of rainfall. Where there is at least 35 to 55 inches (89 to 140 cm) of rain annually, grass, fire-resistant shrubs, and tall deciduous trees create savanna woodlands. Areas that receive less rain, about 20 to 35 inches (50 to 89 cm) a year, are savanna grasslands, with grasses, low shrubs, and a scattering of small deciduous trees.

Background Information *(cont.)*

Steppe

Away from the equator, the savanna climate of the north and south blends into the drier steppe climate zone. Here the rainfall, which averages between 10 and 20 inches (25 and 50 cm), is concentrated in one season.

Because of the lower rainfall, the steppe vegetation has a thinner grass covering than the savanna and scattered succulent or semi-succulent trees. Unlike hardwoods, these plants can store water in their fleshy leaves or thorns to assure their survival in the dry season.

Desert

Africa has more arid, or desert, climate zones than any other continent. The Sahara in the north, the Horn Desert in the east, and the Kalahari and Namib deserts in the southwest have less than 10 inches (25 cm) of yearly rainfall. In the Sahara both the daily and seasonal temperatures show extreme variation. The average July temperature is more than 90° F (32.2° C). The nighttime temperature in the cold season often drops below 32° F° (0° C).

Some desert areas, where the annual rainfall is less than 5 inches (13 cm), have only sparse vegetation or none at all. Areas that receive 5 to 12 inches (13 to 30 cm) of rain a year often have a covering of grasses and scattered low shrubs. This is known as a scrub zone. In some places, deep springs rise to the desert surface, creating fertile oases where date palms, orange trees, and a form of acacia grow. Manmade water wells, some more than 3,280 feet (1000 m) deep, form artificial oases.

Mediterranean

The climate of the extreme northwest and the extreme southwest of Africa is similar to the climate of other Mediterranean countries, with mild, wet winters and warm, dry summers.

A variety of trees and plants grow under these conditions, including date palms, orange trees, and cotton plants.

Mountain Forest

Some countries of eastern Africa, like Kenya and Uganda, as well as portions of Cameroon, Angola, and Ethiopia, have consistent temperatures and rainfall throughout the year. Because they are at higher elevations, on high plateaus or mountains, the climate is often more temperate. Near the equator, the rainfall may be only slightly less than in the tropical rain forests.

At these elevations, the ground covering of shrubs gives way to oil palms, hardwood trees, and primitive conifers.

Vegetation Zones of Africa

The vegetation zones of Africa range from semibarren to lush rain forest. Rainfall and temperature determine the vegetation, wildlife, natural resources, agriculture, lifestyle, and even the history of each region of Africa.

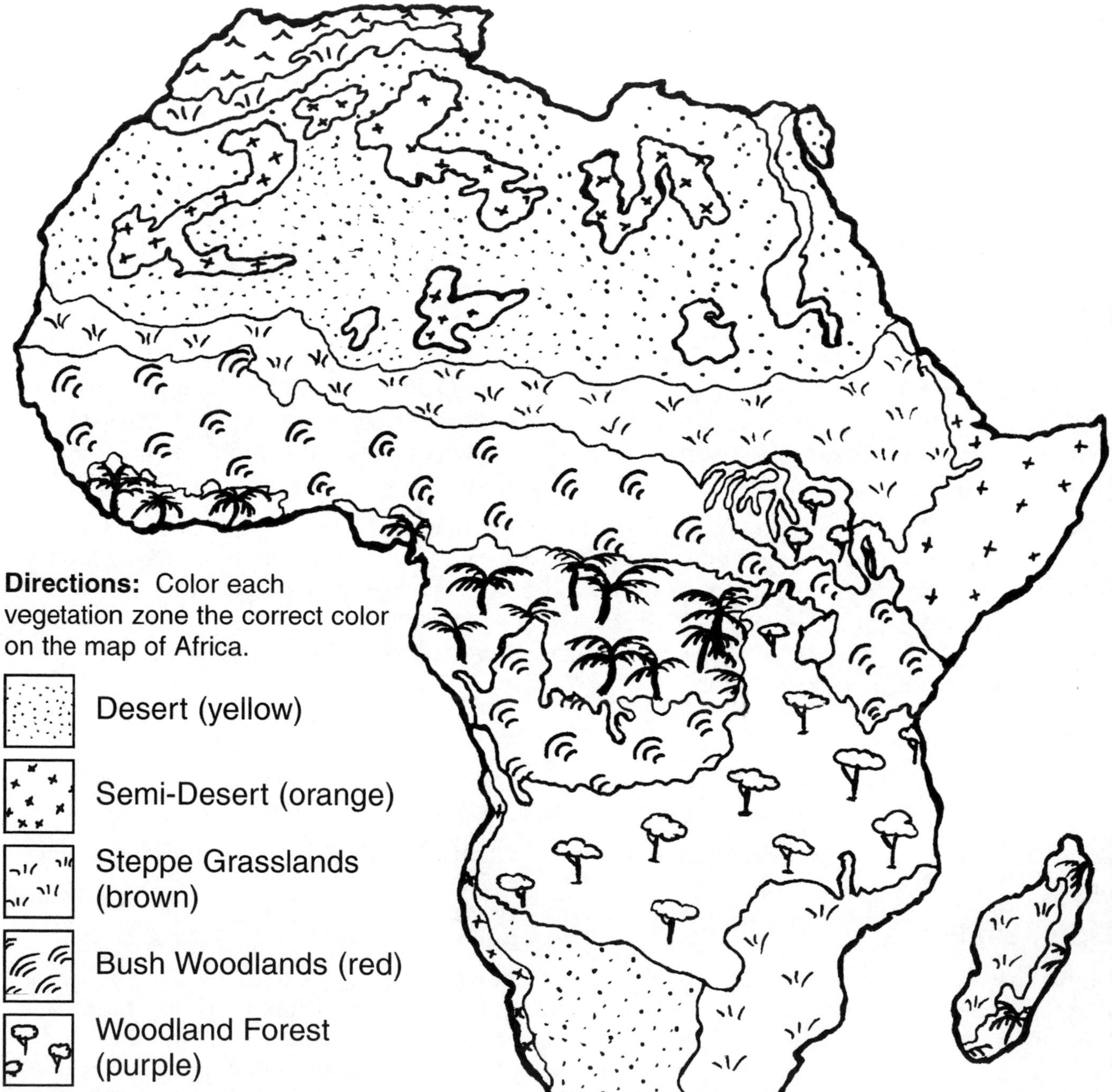

Directions: Color each vegetation zone the correct color on the map of Africa.

Desert (yellow)

Semi-Desert (orange)

Steppe Grasslands (brown)

Bush Woodlands (red)

Woodland Forest (purple)

Tropical Rain Forest (dark green)

Mediterranean and Cape (blue)

Major Rivers of Africa

In Africa the major rivers are like highways for travel and trade by boat. Rivers also provide water for plants, animals, and people. Most cities in Africa are found near rivers or coastline.

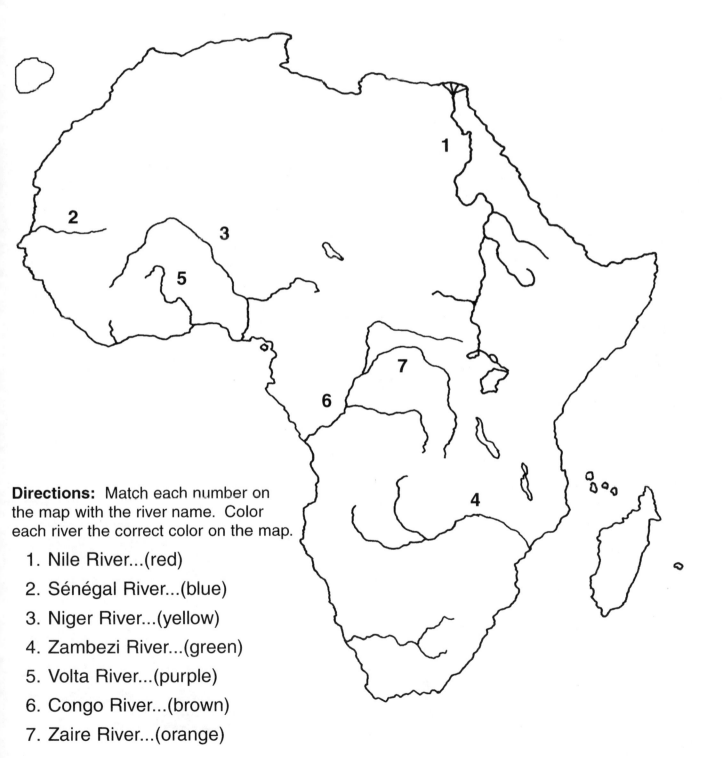

Directions: Match each number on the map with the river name. Color each river the correct color on the map.

1. Nile River...(red)
2. Sénégal River...(blue)
3. Niger River...(yellow)
4. Zambezi River...(green)
5. Volta River...(purple)
6. Congo River...(brown)
7. Zaire River...(orange)

75

Bird-of-Paradise

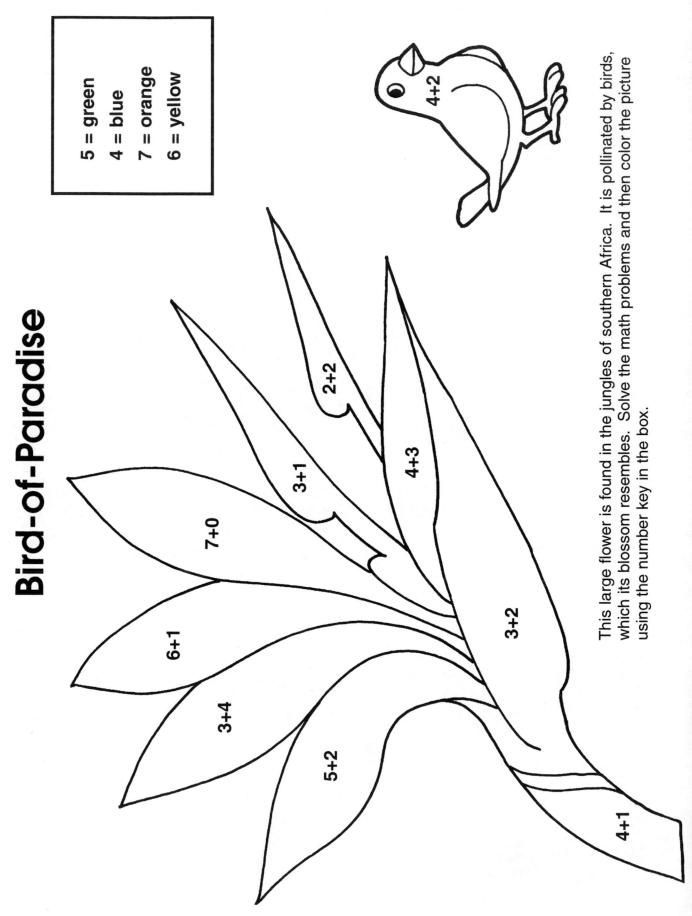

5 = green	
4 = blue	
7 = orange	
6 = yellow	

4+2

2+2

3+1

4+3

7+0

6+1

3+4

3+2

5+2

4+1

This large flower is found in the jungles of southern Africa. It is pollinated by birds, which its blossom resembles. Solve the math problems and then color the picture using the number key in the box.

Trees of the Rain Forest

In the rain forest trees grow tall, looking for the sun. Their leaves form a cover called the canopy. The canopy keeps the forest shady and cool. Many animals and birds make their homes in the trees.

You can make a pull-up tree.

Materials

- newspaper
- scissors
- ruler
- green tempera paint
- tape
- coffee can

Directions

1. Place one sheet of newspaper on top of another. Starting at the short side, roll the newspaper into a tube about 2 inches (5 cm) in diameter. Place a piece of tape at the middle and the bottom of the tube.

2. Make four cuts each about six inches (15 cm) long into the top of the tube.

3. Reach inside and gently pull the inside up and out.

4. Paint your finished tree.

5. Add a bird, butterfly, or brightly colored flower to decorate your tree.

6. Stand your tree in the coffee can. Use crumpled newspaper to secure it.

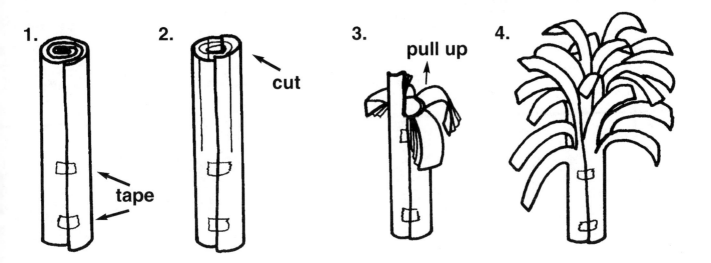

Use the completed trees to create a rain forest scene. Make more trees in different heights to represent bushes, shrubs, smaller trees, etc. Bring in some stuffed animals of the type that live in the rain forest.

African

Wildlife

Background Information

The African continent is the home of many different kinds of animals. While some are similar to animals found in other countries, a large number of them are unique to the African continent. From the lush tropical rain forest to the barren desert lands, each species is uniquely adapted to its native habitat. The number and type of animals in a region depend on the climatic conditions and vegetation in each region.

Rain Forest

The gorilla, the largest ape in the world, makes its home in the dense vegetation of the tropical rain forest. Chimpanzees build nests in the trees of the rain forest. Many types of monkeys, as well as flying squirrels, bats, and lemurs, inhabit the tall trees. One of the most unusual African rain forest animals is the okapi. Unknown by the outside world until 1901, the okapi was at first thought to be a form of zebra because of its striped legs. The okapi, however, resembles the fossils of early giraffes and is classified as a member of the giraffe family. Below the canopy of tall trees, the rain forest teems with insects, including ants, termites, and mosquitoes. Brightly colored tropical birds and butterflies are also at home in the rain forest.

Tropical Savannah

The sweeping grasslands and woodlands of the tropical savannah attract a wide variety of animals. Herds of herbivores like deer, zebras, African elephants, buffaloes, and giraffes graze the savannahs, migrating as the supply of food is exhausted or the seasons change. Several species of antelope, including gnus (also called wildebeests), impalas, and gazelles, make their homes in these areas. Impalas are known for their great ability to leap or jump when threatened. Rhinoceroses and hippopotamuses favor areas near lakes and rivers. Carnivores also abound in the savannahs. Lions, leopards, cheetahs, mongooses, jackals, and hyenas hunt and prey on the grazing herds. They, too, migrate, following their food sources.

Deserts

The fennec fox, or desert fox, is adapted to the harsh desert environment. It is more active at night. During the day it burrows into the desert sand. Along with the jerboa, a leaping rodent, the fennec fox is able to survive without drinking water. Other desert dwellers include hares and gazelles. Hyenas and jackals often prey on other animals of the desert. The best-known desert animals are the camels used to transport goods and people across the sands of the desert. Camels are domesticated animals. Like the smaller desert dwellers, the camel has adapted to the lack of moisture. The extra fat stored in the camel's hump provides the water needed for survival.

Mediterranean Coast

North of the Sahara and along the northwestern coast, animal life is similar to that of Eurasia. Sheep, goats, horses, and camels are common. Barbary sheep, African red deer, and two types of ibex are native to the northern African coast.

Background Information (cont.)

Birds

Most birds of Africa are similar to species found in Eurasia. Several types of guinea fowl, a species related to the familiar peacock, are indigenous to Africa and are the leading game birds. Pelicans, Goliath herons, flamingos, storks, and egrets can be found in great numbers in coastal regions, river areas, and lakes. The ibis, a bird sacred to ancient Egypt, is common in the Nile region, and the ostrich inhabits eastern and southern Africa.

Reptiles

Reptiles commonly found in Africa include lizards, crocodiles, and tortoises. Many different venomous snakes, including the mamba, live in sub-Saharan Africa. Constricting snakes include pythons, which are found mainly in western Africa, and boa constrictors, a species indigenous only to Madagascar.

Modern-Day Safari

Once an African safari meant hunting and shooting animals for sport. Today many tourists make safaris in the game sanctuaries of Africa armed only with cameras. The tourists camp in lodges or tents and take home photographs of the animals.

Game sanctuaries in Africa can be divided into two types, national parks and game reserves. The national parks are areas where the wildlife, animals, and natural habitat are protected. No people are allowed to live there. On the game reserves the animals and the natural habitat are also protected, but some people are allowed to live there as well. By protecting the habitat of these animals from destruction by humans, future generations will be allowed to share the natural treasures of this great continent.

Some of Africa's game sanctuaries are listed below. Students may want to write letters to these parks to receive information about the animals there.

Zambia:	Victoria Falls National Park (ape refuges)
Ghana:	Tano Nimri Forest Preserve
Kenya:	Aberdare National Park (also Treetops Hotel, game-viewing station), Masai Amboseli Game Reserve at the base of Mt. Kilamanjaro, Masai Mara Game Reserve, Mount Kenya National Park, Nairobi National Park, Tsavo National Park
Uganda:	Murchison Falls National Park, Valley National Park
Tanzania:	Ngorongoro Conservation Area (controlled land use area, water resources, forests, wildlife, controlled and managed gardening and grazing)
South Africa:	Addo Elephant National Park, Kalahari Gemsbo National Park, Kruger National Park (Sabi Reserve in South Africa became the Kruger National Park and serves as a prototype of many of the parks that have been established on the continent.)

Endangered Species

Many of the unique animals of the African continent are considered to be endangered species, including gorillas, African elephants, and rhinoceroses. Some have been hunted to near extinction for their pelts, horns, or tusks. Others have slowly disappeared as settlements encroach on savannahs. Slash and burn farming of fragile rain forest environments and disruptions in normal weather patterns also have taken a toll on animal populations. Laws now protect many endangered species, and the possession or sale of any part of an endangered animal is a criminal offense.

80

Identifying African Animals

The information and activities below can be used in a number of different ways to reinforce the students' knowledge about African wildlife.

Suggested Activities

- Have students color the pictures on page 82–84. Cut the pages apart on the solid lines. Fold each strip in half and paste the description to the back of the picture. As an alternative, cut the pictures and descriptions apart and paste them on construction paper to make a book.

- Read about African animals in books or on the Internet. Add one interesting fact to each description.

- Provide blank cards and ask the students to find two more interesting African animals.

- Play charades. Ask each student to act out the role of an animal while the others try to guess who he or she is.

- Play a guessing game. Have each student prepare and read a clue based on an animal description. He or she then asks "Who am I?"

- Play 20 questions. Secretly assign an animal to each student. He or she will answer "yes" or "no" to questions posed by classmates until they have enough information to guess the identity.

- Play concentration. Make copies of pages 82–84. Cut the pictures and descriptions apart. Group the students in pairs to match descriptions with pictures.

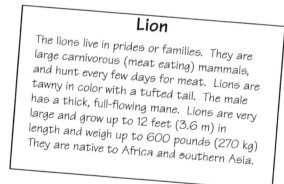

Lion

The lions live in prides or families. They are large carnivorous (meat eating) mammals, and hunt every few days for meat. Lions are tawny in color with a tufted tail. The male has a thick, full-flowing mane. Lions are very large and grow up to 12 feet (3.6 m) in length and weigh up to 600 pounds (270 kg) They are native to Africa and southern Asia.

- Ask the students to sort the animals by habitat (rain forest, savannah, etc.).

- Ask the students to sort the cards by the animals' diets.

- Have the students research which of their animals are endangered species and tell why they are endangered.

- Have the students locate the animals' native regions on a map.

- Present an animal masquerade parade. The people of Africa often feature animals in their celebrations. Ask the children to each choose their favorite animal. Have them each create a mask, headdress, or costume that represents the animal that they have chosen. As an extension, ask each child why he or she chose that particular animal.

Identifying African Animals *(cont.)*

Lion

The lions live in prides or families. They are large carnivorous (meat eating) mammals, and hunt every few days for meat. Lions are tawny in color with a tufted tail. The male has a thick, full-flowing mane. Lions are very large and grow up to 12 feet (3.6 m) in length and weigh up to 600 pounds (270 kg) They are native to Africa and southern Asia.

Elephant

The elephants live in large herds ruled by female leaders. Elephants are the largest land animals, standing 9–12 feet (2.7–3.6 m) tall and weighing 5–6 tons (4,500–5,400 kg). The elephant is very smart. The African elephant has larger ears and looser skin than the Indian elephant. African elephants can not easily be tamed in the way Indian elephants can be.

Rhinoceros

The rhinoceros has thick gray or blackish skin. It lives near water. It has sharp horns that help it to fight. This animal weighs from two to three and one-half tons. The rhinoceros is hunted for its horns and is endangered. The rhinoceros is a native to Africa and southeastern Asia.

Gnu

Also called the wildebeest, this is one of the many African antelopes. The Gnus has a broad, smooth horns that curve downward, outward, and then upward. Its horns and shaggy face make it look fierce. Gnus can run very fast. Their home is in the grasslands of Southern Africa.

82

Identifying African Animals *(cont.)*

Giraffe

The giraffe is the tallest living animal. It has a very long neck and long forelegs. It can stand 18 to 20 feet (5.5 to 6 m) tall. Giraffes are light tan in color. Their long necks help them to reach up in tall trees to eat the leaves. The giraffes serve as "lookouts" for some animals as they eat.

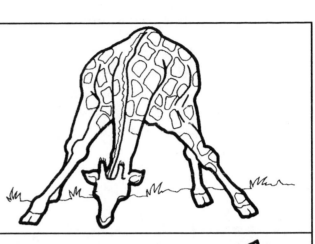

Zebra

Zebras are swift-running mammals of southern and eastern Africa. They are covered with alternating black and white or brown and buff stripes. The zebra's bold stripes help it hide in the trees and tall grass. They are rarely domesticated.

Gorilla

Gorillas live in family groups in the jungle. They eat fruits, bamboo shoots, leaves, and vegetables. Gorillas stand up to 6 feet (720 cm) tall and have very long arms and strong jaws. Their faces are covered with shiny black skin.

Okapi

This mammal has striped legs like a zebra but belongs to the same animal family as the giraffe. It eats leaves and lives deep in the rain forest.

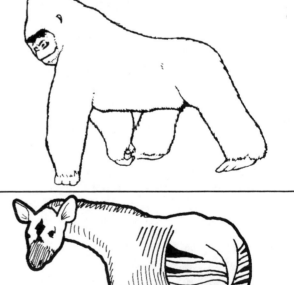

Identifying African Animals *(cont.)*

Fennec Fox

The fennec is the smallest member of the fox family. It lives in the Sahara desert and eats plants, insects, and small animals. Its big ears help it stay cool in the heat of the day.

Camel

This mammal came to Africa from Asia 2,000 years ago and is still used to travel through the desert regions. A camel can eat tough spiny plants and can go for a long period of time without drinking water. A thirsty camel can drink 35 gallons (135 L) of water in six minutes.

Warthog

Warthogs are members of the pig family. They have two sets of tusks and two sets of growths that resemble warts on their heads. They have stocky bodies with thin legs and long, tufted tails. Warthogs are common on the plains and in the open woodlands of Africa. Their diet includes grass, berries, bark, roots, and the remains of dead animals.

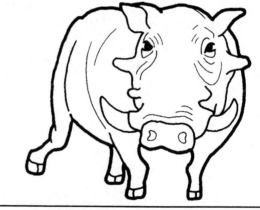

Chimpanzee

Chimpanzees prefer to live in or near trees in equatorial Africa. They avoid direct sunlight and build sleeping nests in the treetops. Chimpanzees eat about 200 kinds of leaves and fruit, termites, ants, honey, birds' eggs, birds, and small mammals.

Animal Patterns

Animals in Africa have patterns of colors on their fur for camouflage. Color the correct pattern on the leopard, zebra, and giraffe.

Jungle Camouflage

Some animals are hiding in this scene. Can you find them? Color each animal you find. Write the animal names on the lines below the picture.

Learn to Draw the King of the Jungle

Look at each picture below. Follow the steps to draw your own lion in the box provided.

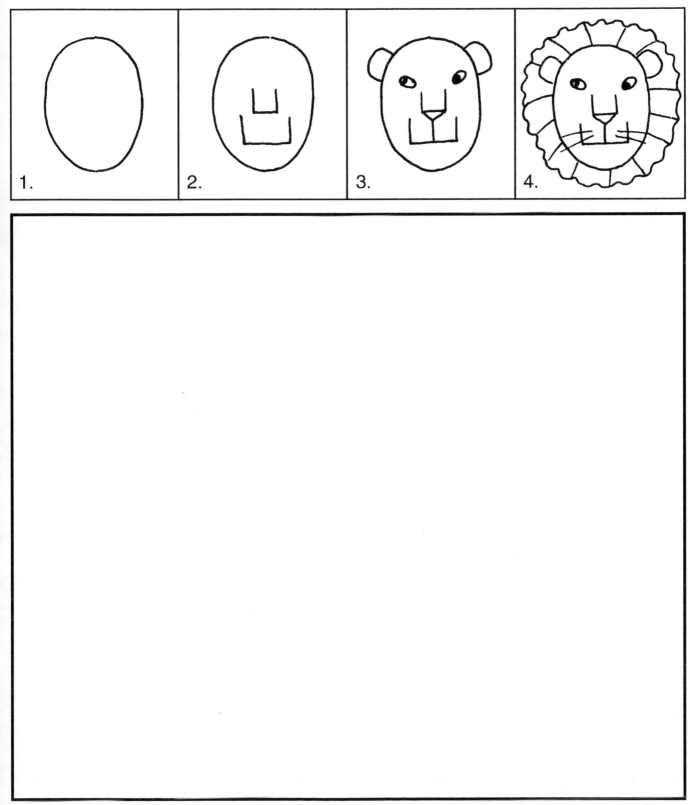

1.

2.

3.

4.

Panther in the Grass

The panther is a black leopard with black spots and green eyes. The panther hunts on the African savannah. Draw what the panther is looking at as it hides in the grass.

African Rain Forest

Directions: Draw your favorite rain forest animal. Color your rain forest picture.

Savanna Grasslands of Africa

See page 91 for directions.

Savanna Animals of Africa

The savanna grasslands of Africa are home to many animals that graze and hunt there. Color each animal. Cut out the savanna animals and place them in the picture on page 90.

Monkey Tree

Monkeys live in the jungles of Africa. They find food and safety in the trees. Color the tree and monkeys. Cut out the monkeys and paste them in the tree.

92

Draw an Animal Mask

The Bobo people of Mali carve and paint wooden masks of animals. Draw and color your own animal mask next to the Bobo mask.

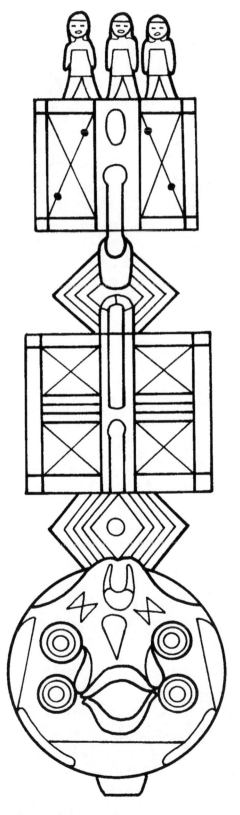

Zingy Zebra Lives in Africa

Zebras have stripes that help them hide in the tall grasses in Africa. The stripes appear in many variations. As you make Zingy Zebra, you can create the stripes in your own way.

Materials

- 9" x 12" (23 x 30 cm) white construction paper
- 8" x 12" (20 x 30 cm) black construction paper
- 9" (23 cm) piece of black yarn
- copies of page 95
- crayons
- glue

Directions

1. Fold a sheet of white construction paper in half lengthwise.
2. Draw a half circle on the side opposite the fold.
3. Hold the fold and cut the half circle from the open side.
4. Cut out stripes from the black construction paper.
5. Glue stripes on both sides of the zebra body.
6. Color the stripes on the head pattern black.
7. Cut out the head.
8. Fold the head on the fold line and glue it to the inside of the zebra's body.
9. Make a tail by cutting several strands of yarn and knotting them at one end. Glue the knotted end to the zebra as shown.

Steps 1 and 2

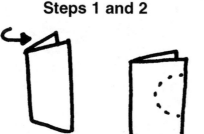

Step 3

Steps 4 and 5

Steps 8 and 9

Zingy Zebra Lives in Africa *(cont.)*

Directions

1. Color the stripes black.
2. Cut along the dotted line.
3. Fold the head in half as shown.
4. Attach the head to the zebra body.

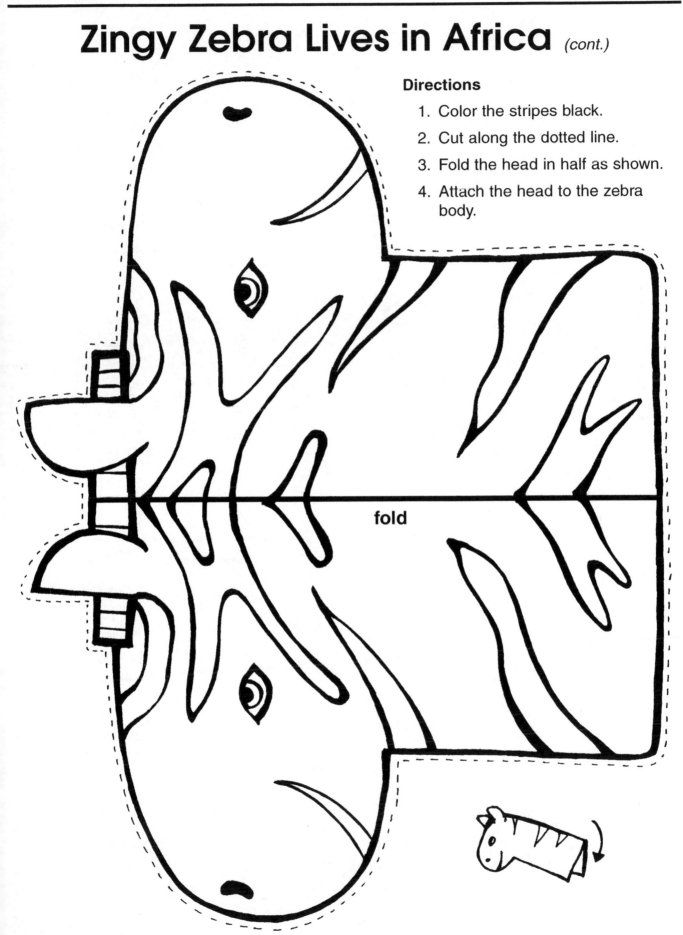

fold

Where Do Animals Live?

Some animals live only in the tropical forest, and others live only in the savanna grasslands. A very few live in the desert. One reason for this is the food that each kind of animal prefers. Draw a line from each animal below to its habitat.

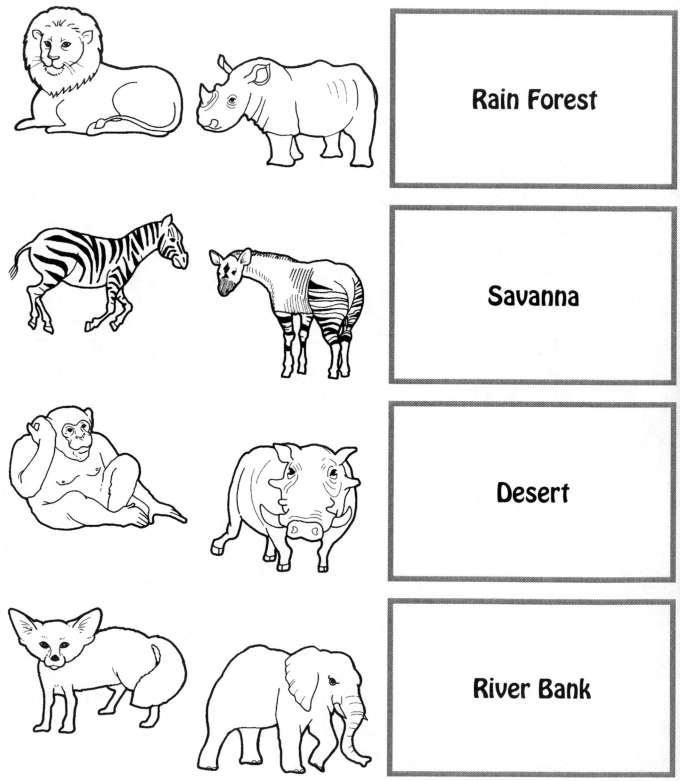

Rain Forest

Savanna

Desert

River Bank

96

Who Am I? Crossword

Read the clues below to decide where the animal names belong in the puzzle. Choose from the names in the box.

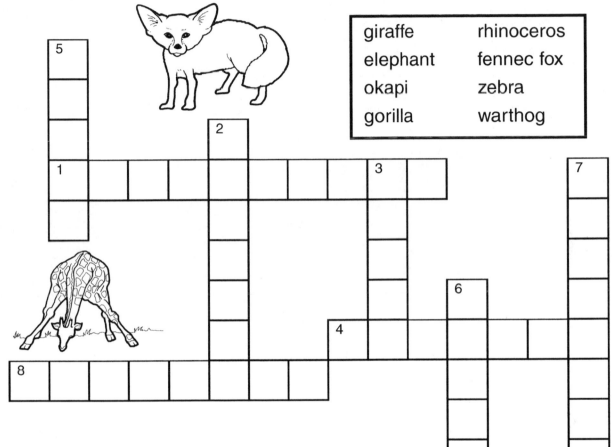

giraffe	rhinoceros
elephant	fennec fox
okapi	zebra
gorilla	warthog

Across

1. I weigh a couple of tons and have thick gray skin. My biggest features are my sharp horns.

4. I am the tallest living animal and have a very long neck.

8. I live in a large herd and am the biggest land animal who stands 9–12 feet tall.

Down

2. I live in the jungle with my family. I am very tall and have shiny black skin on my face.

3. Some say I have stripes like a zebra, but actually, I am a closer relative to the giraffe.

5. I have black and white stripes that help me hide in the trees.

6. I am a close relative to the pig. I have a stocky body and a long tufted tail.

7. I am the smallest member of the fox family. Because I live in the Sahara Desert, I use my big ears to help me stay cool.

People

of

Africa

Background Information

The diversity of the African continent extends to the people of Africa. More than 3,000 distinct ethnic groups, each with its own unique culture, traditions, history, and lifestyle have been identified. Over 1,000 languages and dialects are spoken.

Ancient Cultures

Human beings have lived in Africa for at least 50,000 years. Archaeologists have found evidence that organized communities of farmers and herders existed in Africa beginning about 5,000 B.C.

Egypt

Among the earliest known settlements in Africa were those in the fertile Nile valley. By the year 3000 B.C., a strong political system under a single ruler united the people of the Nile valley. The Egyptian civilization prospered and dominated much of northern Africa and the surrounding Mediterranean area. Today people marvel at the massive monuments like the pyramids and the Sphinx, which have endured in the desert for centuries. Throughout its long history, Egypt has been conquered several times. In the seventh century it fell to the Arabs, who introduced Islam and the Arabic language. In the late twentieth century Egypt continues to play an important role in the politics of the region.

Kush

The Kush people, also known as Nubians, lived in the area that is now called Sudan. Historians suggest that the Kush were a wealthy and powerful people, farmers and herders who traded with the ancient Egyptians. In about 767 B.C., the Kush army conquered Egypt. Overthrown by the Assyrians in 671 B.C., the Kush people retreated to their ancient land. Their empire lasted until A.D. 200. By the beginning of the sixth century, the Kush culture had disappeared. Legends of the Ashanti and Yoruba people suggest that Kushites migrated to West Africa to found new empires.

Nok

The oldest culture in West Africa, the Nok, is known only from artifacts recovered by archaeologists. The evidence suggests that these were an agricultural society who lived in villages. Their houses were made of branches and dried mud. In addition to farming, the Nok mined the rich gold deposits of the area. Terracotta statues indicate that the Nok people were interested in art. These people lived in the area now known as Nigeria from about 500 B.C. until A.D. 200. Hunting and herding societies began to control the Nok region, establishing their own agricultural communities. The Nok were assimilated, and their culture disappeared.

Background Information *(cont.)*

Ghana

Ghana, the first great civilization south of the Sahara, occupied the present-day country of Mali. Ghana rose to power in the sixth century. In the medieval era, universities flourished, and students from Asia and Europe studied philosophy, medicine, and law. The people were farmers, gold miners, and ironsmiths. Located on a trading crossroad, Ghanians levied taxes to control traders and engaged in commerce with many other nations. Known for its large, stone cities, Ghana was seized in 1203 by the King of Sosso. The Ghana culture faded after its capital city was destroyed by the King of Mali in 1240.

Mali

This empire, established in the early 1200s, was larger than all of Europe. It contained the countries now known as Mali, Mauritania, and Senegal. The economy of Mali was based on farming, herding, and mining salt, gold, and copper. The most famous city in Mali was its cultural center, Timbuktu. For a time, Mali was known in both the Middle East and Europe as a rich and splendid kingdom. In the 1400s Mali declined and was divided into several smaller kingdoms. Eventually what remained of the Mali culture became part of the Mandinka kingdoms.

Songhai

This empire reached from the Atlantic coast to what is now Niger and Nigeria. The Songhai people gained control of Mali and then went on to conquer other neighboring people. As the empire grew, many people turned from their traditional occupations of farming, fishing, and shipbuilding to trading in the markets. Salt and gold mines created wealth for many. Well-armed Moroccan troops captured the key cities of Timbuktu and Gao in 1591 and claimed control of the gold and salt mines. The Songhai empire crumbled and was absorbed by the Hausa, Fulani, and Bambara empires.

Modern Cultures

Until the 16th century, much of Africa was unknown to and unexplored by Europeans. As interest and knowledge of Africa and its riches grew in the 18th and 19th centuries, many countries, including France, Britain, Holland, Belgium, Spain, and Germany, established colonies in Africa. They did so without regard for the traditional boundaries of the native ethnic groups. In the middle of the 20th century, the native Africans sought their independence and established new governments. These new countries have within their borders diverse native ethnic groups. Each ethnic group has its own traditions, language, and culture.

The extended family is the basic social unit of most of these peoples. In African tradition each family is part of a larger society formed of kin groups such as lineages and clans. A village is frequently composed of a single kin group related by a single line of descent, either male or female.

Make a 3-D Pyramid

Color and cut out the
pyramid, palm trees, and
camel. Fold and tape as
shown.

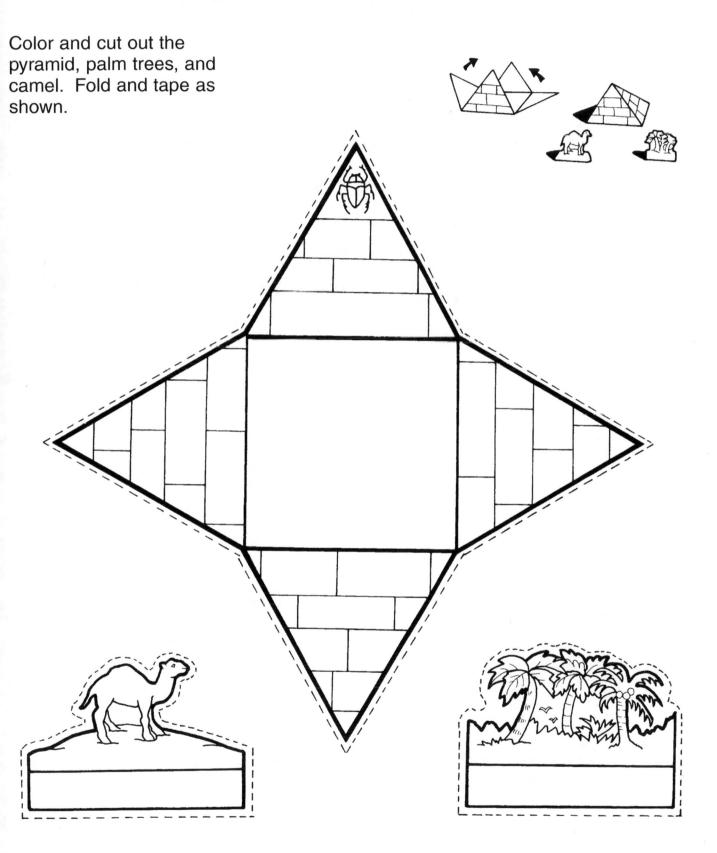

The Hieroglyphic Alphabet

In ancient Egypt the people used a form of picture writing called hieroglyphics (hi-row-glif-ics). They used this writing to carve the name of a king or queen inside of an oval frame called a cartouche. They believed that this provided magical protection for the person.

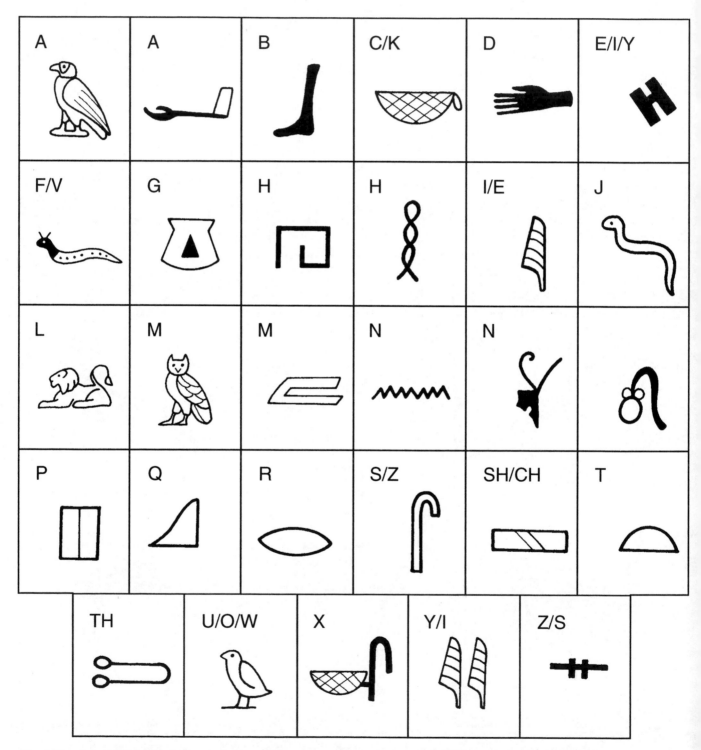

Find the hieroglyphic letters that spell your name and cut them out. Paste them inside the cartouche on page 103.

Cartouche

Use crayons to add color to the cartouche. Paste the hieroglyphic letters of your name in the open space.

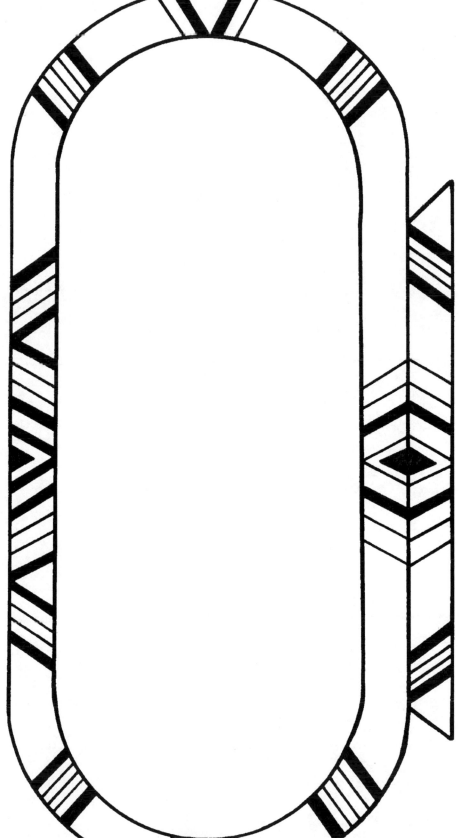

Pyramid Shape Book

1. Color the eye of Horus

2. Cut out the pyramid cover.

3. Use the cover as a pattern to cut writing paper pages in the same pyramid shape.

4. Place writing pages behind the cover.

5. Fold the tab behind the pages.

6. Staple the book pages to the cover along the left side of the pyramid.

7. Write some facts or a story about ancient Egypt. Write your name and the title of your book on the book cover.

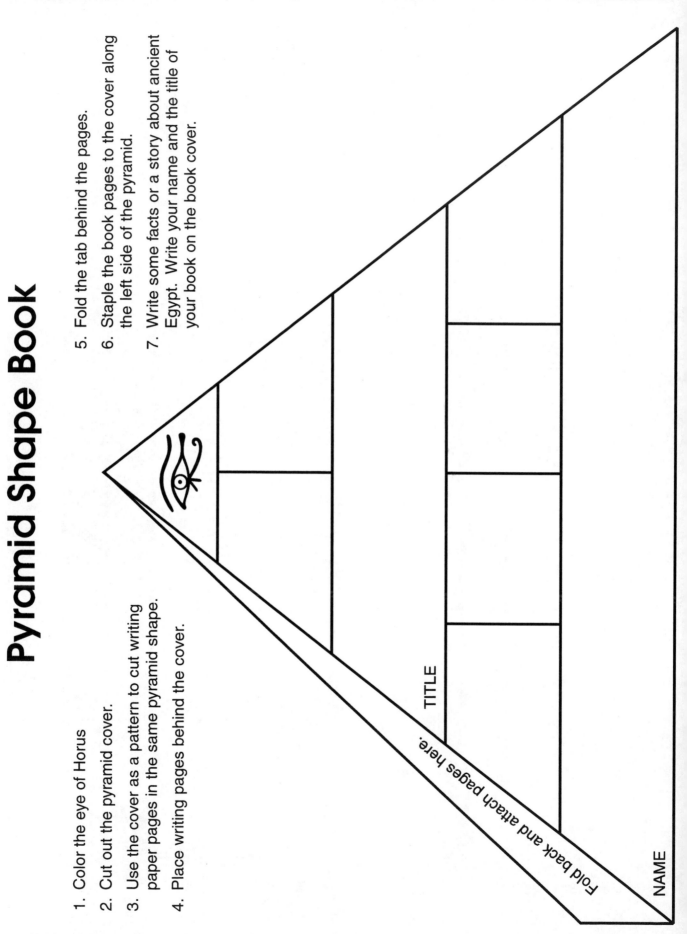

Fold back and attach pages here.

TITLE

NAME

Homes and Lifestyles

Background Information

The contrasts seen throughout the African continent extend to the homes and lifestyles of the various people. In many areas there are large cities that show the influence of the European colonists. There are also many ethnic groups, sometimes called tribes, each with its own unique history and traditions which follow traditional African lifestyles.

Hunter-Gatherers

Anthropologists tell us that the earliest people depended entirely on the environment for food and shelter. More than 3,000 years ago these early people developed a lifestyle based on hunting wild game, fishing, and gathering fruit, nuts, edible roots, and vegetables. Hunter-gatherers lead a nomadic lifestyle. As food sources were exhausted or game migrated, the people followed them, traveling in small family units. Much of their time was spent in pursuit of food. Men tracked and killed game to provide meat and skins for clothing. No part of the animal was wasted. Women and children picked fruits and vegetables and dug for edible roots. Once there must have been thousands of hunter-gatherers across the African continent.

Today there are only a few people who follow this simple lifestyle. The San people once roamed over much of southern Africa. Driven out of their traditional territory, about 2,000 members of the San continue to follow their traditional lifestyle in the eastern Kalahari Desert. In that harsh environment, the nomadic bands of San people move about once a month. Their possessions and clothing are few and simple. Called Bushmen by the white settlers of South Africa, the San are also called Khoisan. They speak many different dialects of the click language family.

The Mbuti people live in the Ituri Forest of the Congo. Long ago the Greeks used the word pygmy, which means a small unit of measure, to describe these small people. Although the Mbuti have interacted with other native ethnic groups and with European explorers, most of them follow their traditional lifestyle. They live in small camps in the forest. Each family has a dome-shaped hut made of branches and leaves. When the vegetation is used up, they move to another location in the forest.

Herders and Planters

Over time, some of the ethnic groups turned to herding, raising cattle, sheep, and goats for their own use, and to planting crops. These new lifestyles guaranteed a food source for the people and allowed them to establish more permanent settlements. Finding sufficient food was no longer their sole occupation and members of the community could devote time to different occupations. Because there was more food, these societies expanded, moving into new areas as their need for land increased.

The Maasai of Kenya and Tanzania are herders who rely almost exclusively on cattle for their food supply. The Tuareg of northern Africa began raising and herding camels almost 2,000 years ago. As they migrated through the desert regions, they became traders, as well. Today some of the Tuareg people follow the traditional life of herding and trading while others have become farmers.

Background Information *(cont.)*

A Place to Call Home

Africa is a huge continent with a variety of architectural styles. The homes, schools, stores, churches, mosques, and temples of each country feature elements of design and decor that are unique to that country. However, the love of graceful design and bright colors is evident throughout African architecture. Intricate patterns are often carved and painted on doorways, support beams, and walls. The family members themselves often make beautiful furniture, utensils, and household objects that are used in everyday life. The family is the focus of the cultures of Africa, and the home is a source of pride, identity, and comfort to each family.

Traditional African Homes

Materials used for housing vary depending on climate, available building materials, and lifestyle. The size of the apartment, house, or family compound depends on the wealth of the family and the number of family members. Some homes are very large, with tiled walls and courtyard gardens decorated with fountains and flowers. Other homes are very small, nestled into the forest trees. Some homes are even built on sticks in the middle of a lake. These homes can only be reached by boat.

Desert dwellers such as the Tuareg traditionally travel with tents made of woven wool which are rolled up into a bundle and carried on the back of the camel or horse between camps. The people of the equatorial rain forest use large green leaves and reeds to build their small homes. Such temporary homes can be constructed or taken down quickly when it is time for the family group to move to another camp area.

Farmers need to have more permanent homes near their fields. Many of the people of Africa build circular homes from a framework of wood with mud or clay walls and a thatched roof. These materials are readily available in most areas. The traditional thatched roof keeps the home cooler in the day than tin roofing, and it absorbs the heat from the sun and cooking fire, keeping the home warmer at night. In the event that a heavy rain causes damage, the clay bricks and thatched roof can be replaced easily. The families of the entire village gather to help build each home. Men construct the framework, and the women erect the mud-brick or clay walls. There are two kinds of bricks that may be used. Wet bricks are shaped by hand and set directly in place. Dry bricks are made in wooden molds and dried in the sun before being fixed into place with mortar. Once the bricks have been set, they are covered with plaster. Decorative elements are added to the walls and floors.

City Life in Africa

Cities are not new in the history of Africa. Many great cities grew under the old empires. When Europeans established their African colonies, some of these cities were modernized, and others were built. As traditional ways change, more and more people are moving to the cities to find employment, education, and other opportunities. In cities many families live in high-rise apartments or condominiums with modern comforts such as hot and cold running water, electricity, elevators, telephones, TV, computers, and radios. Hospitals, factories, movie theaters, schools, and big department stores make life in the cities easier in many ways. However, the city dwellers also have the headaches of the modern lifestyle, such as traffic jams, overpopulation, crowded streets, and air pollution.

Traditional Home of Burkina Faso

This home is in Burkina Faso, a country in western Africa. Many homes in Africa are made from dried clay and painted by women. The children play in the walled courtyard. Color the picture and then draw a picture of a home and family in your neighborhood.

A Place to Call Home

The people in Africa live in large cities and in small rural villages. Where do you live? Draw a picture of your home. Color the pictures and then cut out the boxes. Do the same on pages 110–112. Put the pages together to make a book. Research to find out more about some of these places.

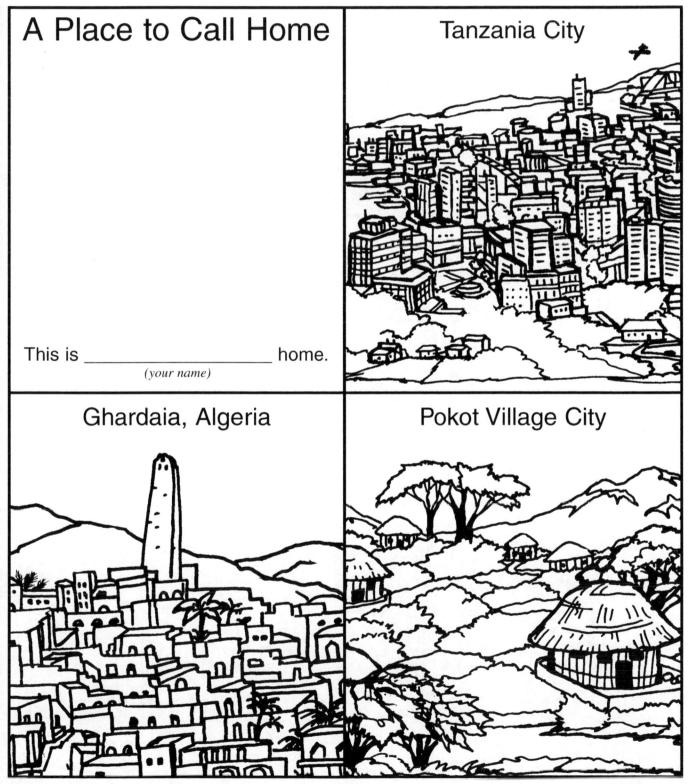

A Place to Call Home

This is _____ home.
(your name)

Tanzania City

Ghardaia, Algeria

Pokot Village City

A Place to Call Home *(cont.)*

See page 109 for directions.

Angola House

Ashanti House

Kamba House

Ndebele House

A Place to Call Home *(cont.)*

See page 109 for directions.

Maasai House

Fon Stilt House

Kenya House

Kikuyu Farmhouse

A Place to Call Home (cont.)

See page 109 for directions.

© Teacher Created Resources, Inc.

Building an African Home

Many traditional buildings in Africa are round. They are built of mud and have thatched roofs made of reeds or grass. Follow the directions to build a traditional African hut.

Materials

- small, round oatmeal boxes
- brown construction paper
- raffia
- crayons or markers
- glue
- scissors
- tape

Directions

1. Cut each oatmeal box in half. (Use one half for each home you make.)	2. Cut a strip of brown construction paper the height of one of the box halves and glue it around the outside.	3. Draw an arched door on the paper. Use crayons or markers to add any decorations.
4. Make a circle for each hut from brown construction paper. The circle should be larger than the base of the oatmeal box.	5. Make a cut as shown in Step 4 and lap the edges to form a cone shape.	6. Tape or glue the roof to the hut. Cut lengths of raffia and glue them in layers on the roof.

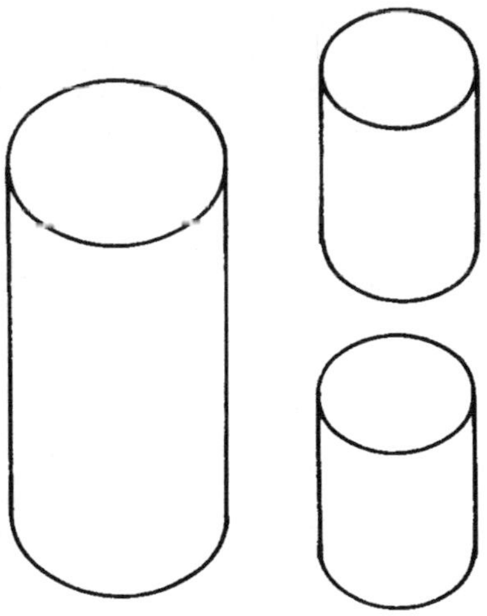

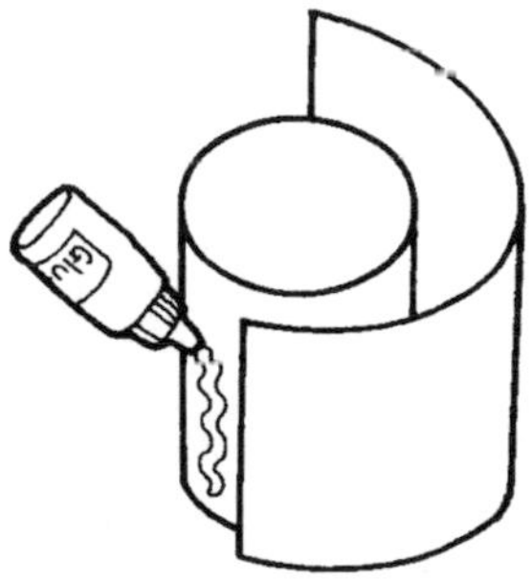

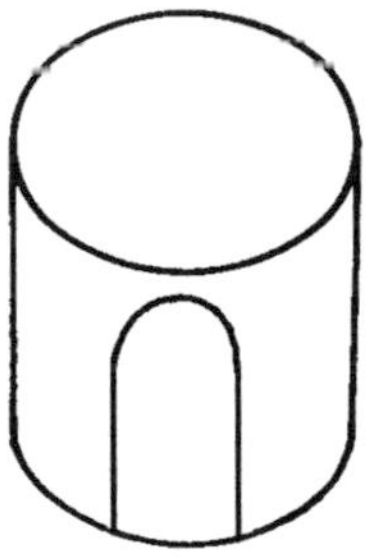

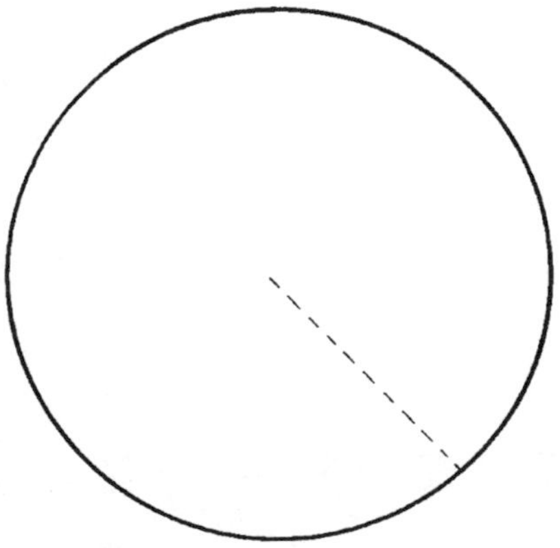

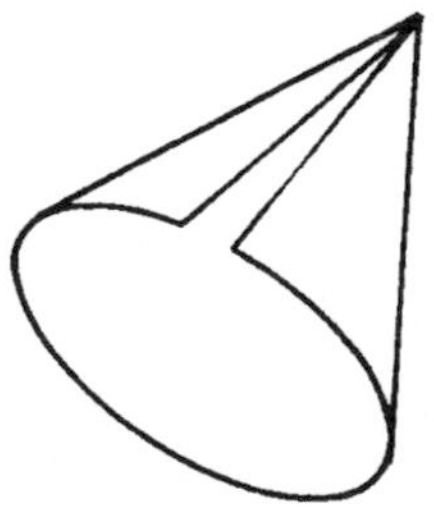

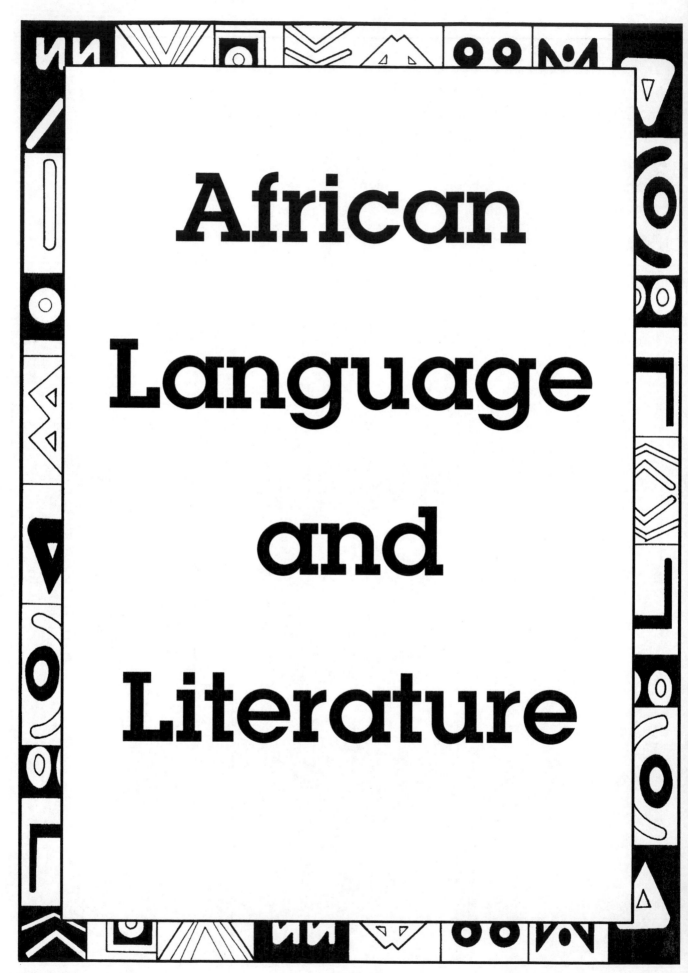

African Language and Literature

Background Information

African Languages

The people of Africa speak many different languages. Each of Africa's ethnic groups has its own language. Because each country in Africa is now home to more than one ethnic group, several languages are spoken in any one country. Many Africans learn to speak two or more languages in order to communicate.

No one is sure exactly how many languages there are in Africa. Scholars estimate that there are between 700 and 3,000 spoken languages on the continent, most with fewer than one million speakers. These languages have been divided into language families based on similarities that indicate a common origin. Studying linguistic patterns and words is a valuable tool in tracing the history of the African people. Some of the African language families are more than 5,000 years old.

The most widely spoken African tongues are Swahili, in eastern and central Africa, and Hausa, which comes from Nigeria in western Africa. Hausa is now used in many parts of Africa, especially for education and trade. Several Hausa newspapers are published, and the body of Hausa literature is growing.

The smallest language family in Africa is the Khoisan group spoken mostly by the Khoikhoi and San peoples of southern Africa. These languages are best known for the unusual click sound given to certain consonants. The sounds are made by a sucking action of the tongue. Changing the position of the tongue and the way air is released into the mouth changes the sound of the clicks. Unused letters like C, Q, X, or special symbols such as \, !, and // are used to write the click consonants. African folk singer Miriam Makeba has recorded a number of traditional songs in the Khoisan languages. Listen to "The Click Song" or another selection from her Africa album.

African Literature

Although the countries of Africa lack written literature, Africa has a rich and varied tradition of oral literature. This oral literature began with the first African societies and continues to prosper today. Proverbs and riddles are told to teach the accepted social codes of conduct, while myths and legends explain the origins and development of states, clans, and other important social organizations as well as teaching a belief in the supernatural. In many instances legends and myths provide extremely accurate accounts of the history of a people. An example is found in the story of Chi Wara, which focuses on the gift of agriculture.

Unlike the legends and myths, which are grounded in fact, folk tales are recognized as fiction. The most famous African folk tales feature the tortoise, hare, and spider. Often the stories tell how these small creatures triumph over larger, stronger animals simply by using intelligence. Anansi is known as a lazy spider who continually finds ways to outsmart others. Magic and flight are also common motifs. It is believed that Aesop drew from traditional African folk tales to create his famous fables. The oral literature of Africa spread to the Caribbean, Latin America, and the United States, traveling with the African people who were sold into slavery. Adapted to reflect a new environment and told in a new language, these ancient stories helped a displaced people maintain their cultural identity.

Many of the traditional stories from Africa have been collected and published. Here is a list of some you might want to read: *Why Mosquitos Buzz in People's Ears* by Verna Aardema (Dial, 1992), *Anansi and the Talking Melon* by Eric A. Krimmel (Holiday House, 1995), and *Anansi the Spider—A Tale from the Ashanti* by Gerald McDermott (Henry Holt, 1987).

Swahili Dictionary

Swahili is a special language spoken by some of the people on the African continent. Cut out the dictionary cover below and the pages that follow to make your own Swahili dictionary. Draw pictures for each of the new words on pages 117–121. When you have finished pages 117–123, put them together with the cover to complete your dictionary.

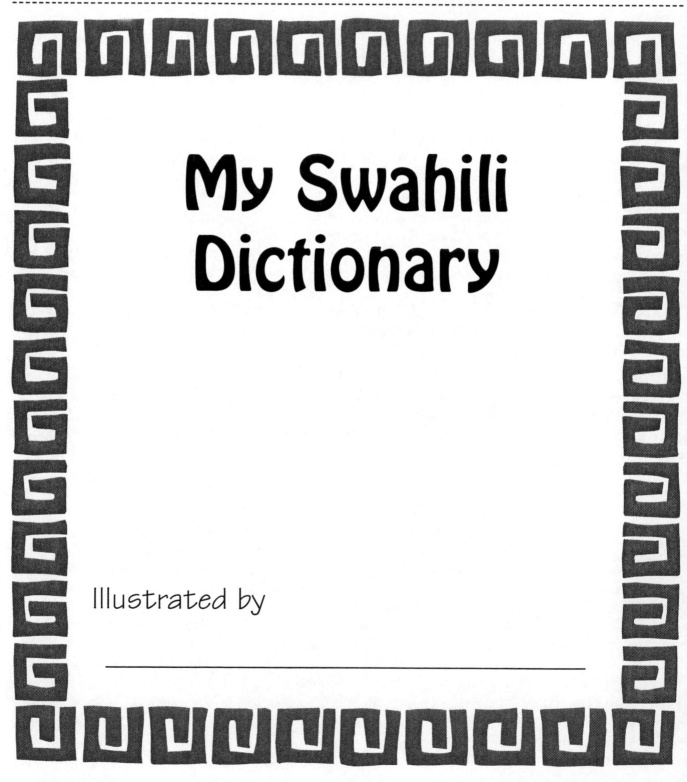

My Swahili Dictionary

Illustrated by

_____

116

Swahili Dictionary (cont.)
People in Africa

See page 116 for directions.

Watoto are children.

Mama means mother.

Swahili Dictionary *(cont.)*
People in Africa

See page 116 for directions.

Rafiki means friend.

Mwalinur is teacher.

Swahili Dictionary (cont.)
Everyday Words in Africa

See page 116 for directions.

Shule is school.

Chakula means food.

Swahili Dictionary *(cont.)*
Everyday Greetings in Africa

See page 116 for directions.

Jambo means hello.

Karibu means welcome.

120

Swahili Dictionary (cont.)
Animal Names in Africa

See page 116 for directions.

Tembo is the elephant.

Punda millia is a zebra.

Swahili Dictionary *(cont.)*
Swahili Number Words

See page 116 for directions.

Write the correct Swahili number word to show how many butterflies there are in each group.

1. moja (MO-jah)
2. Mbili (MM-bee-lee)
3. tatu (TAH-too)
4. nne (NN-nay)
5. tano (TAH-NO)

6. sita (SEE-tah)
7. saba (SAH-bah)
8. nane (NAH-nay)
9. tisa (TEE-sah)
10. kumi (KOO-mee)

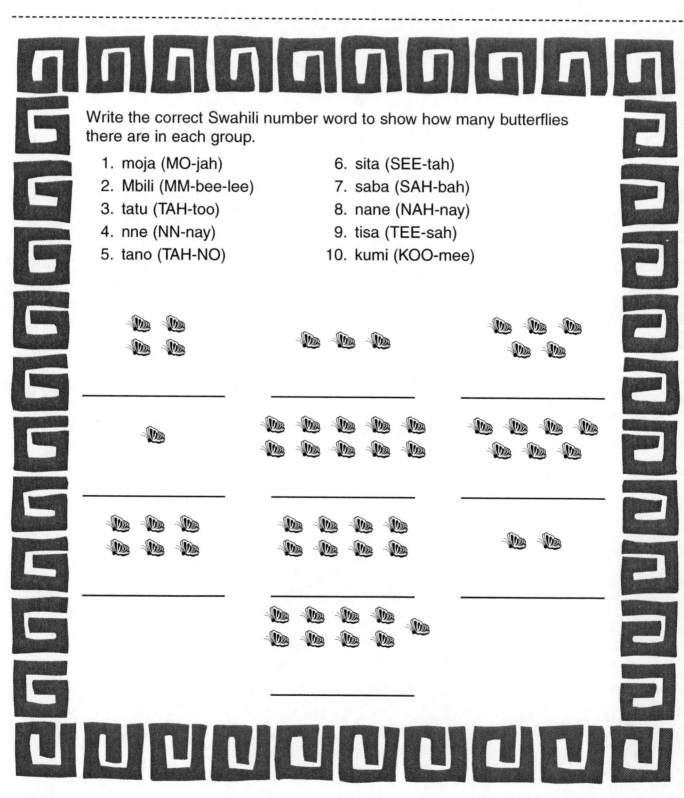

Swahili Dictionary *(cont.)*

Swahili Number Words *(cont.)*

See page 116 for directions.

Use the information from page 122 to write the number word that represents the answer to each of the following picture problems.

kumi   –   saba   = _____

tisa   –   sita   = _____

tano   +   tatu   = _____

moja   +   nne   +   tatu   = _____

tisa   –   saba   = _____

Legends of Africa

The Legend of Chi Wara and the First Farmers

The following story is an original legend from Ghana.

Long ago, in the time of our ancestors, the people did not farm. Family groups hunted in the woods and fished in the rivers. The children gathered wild fruits and nuts from the trees.

Sometimes there was not enough food in the camp area so people would wrap up all of their belongings and travel to a new campsite. They spent many hours each day hunting and gathering food.

One day a strange man named Chi Wara walked out of the woods and surprised two hunters near a lake. The hunters had never seen such a creature before, but they bravely stood and returned his greeting. Chi Wara was part man and part animal. His head looked like an antelope with a nose like an anteater.

Chi Wara made farming tools from stone, wood, and shells. He gave the shovel, adz, and hoe to the hunters. Chi Wara then knelt down and placed a tiny seed in the ground. He watered the seed with a basket of water as he sang a song that no one had ever heard before.

Suddenly a green plant rose from the dark soil. Chi Wara picked the leaves from the plant and gave them to the hunters to eat. The hunters watched and learned. They thanked Chi Wara for sharing his secret with them, for they were to become the first farmers on earth.

The farmers built sturdy houses and stayed in one camp area. They learned how to grow their own food. Now they spent less time hunting and searching for wild fruit and nuts. They had more time to make tools, dance, sing and create art. The farmers were happy.

The descendants of those first farmers continue to farm to this day. At planting and harvest time they celebrate with dance, storytelling, and feasting. Dancers wear special robes and masks to remind them of Chi Wara. "Thank you, Chi Wara, for teaching us your great secret!" The singers call out loud, so he will hear them and bring good crops each year. "Thank you, Chi Wara! We will never forget your kindness!"

124

Legends of Africa *(cont.)*

Chi Wara Antelope Headdress

The Bambara people of Nigeria celebrate planting and harvest of their crops with song and dance. The Chi Wara headdress is worn with a special dance costume. The boys' headdress represents the male antelope and the sun. The girls' headdress shows a baby on the antelope's back. The female represents the earth.

Follow the directions on page 126 to make your own Chi Wara headdress to wear.

male headdress

Legends of Africa *(cont.)*

Chi Wara Antelope Headdress *(cont.)*

Directions: You may choose the female headress below or the male headdress on page 125. Color and cut out the headdress. Fold along the dashed line. Place it on your head with string, as shown below.

female headdress

Legends of Africa *(cont.)*

The Lion's Magic Bones

A very long time ago, Lion was just as fierce as he is today. He went around roaring and eating other animals. Not only was he big and bad, he had wings. His wings were not feathered like a bird's. They were big and strong, made of skin and bones like a bat's wings.

Lion used his wings when he went hunting for food, and no other animals were safe. From up in the sky, Lion could see his whole hunting ground. When he spotted a zebra, a gazelle, or an impala, he would fold his wings and drop on top of his prey. Even the elephants were nervous when they saw Lion's shadow.

Lion's only fear was that someone would break the bones of the animals he had killed. No one knew why this was so, but Lion took special care of the bones. When he finished eating he carefully gathered them, making sure he did not miss any, and carried them to his den.

Just to make sure that no one entered his den while he was hunting, Lion kept a pair of white crows as guards. Of all the crows in the world, only Lion's white crows could talk.

One day, while Lion was on a hunt, Bullfrog hopped up the path to Lion's den.

"Hello, crows," he said. "What do you do here day after day?"

The crows answered, "Watch the bones for Lion. Now go away, Bullfrog."

"Oh," said Bullfrog. "What do the bones do? Is it interesting?"

"No, they just sit," said the crows. "Now go away."

Bullfrog answered, "That seems pretty boring. If you want to stretch your wings, I'll sit here and watch the bones. I can even clean up some of the flies for you."

The crows thought about this. They told each other, "Bullfrog is right. We need to stretch. Lion will never know." So off they flew.

As soon as the crows left, Bullfrog went to work, hopping and hopping on the bones until they were all broken. Bullfrog hopped away from the den.

When the crows came down, they saw what Bullfrog had done and set out to catch him. They dove from the sky to peck Bullfrog, but he made a great leap into the river. The crows landed in the mud on the riverbank.

Bullfrog told them, "If Lion wants to know who broke the bones, tell him I did. He can hunt me here at the dam." Bullfrog dived under the water.

Legends of Africa *(cont.)*

The Lion's Magic Bones *(cont.)*

Meanwhile, Lion had been sitting on a high rock, watching the other animals and deciding what he would like to eat. The gazelles, zebras, wildebeests and giraffes came closer, and Lion lifted his wings to fly, but he could hardly get off the ground. He remembered the bones in his den and roared in anger. The game herd stampeded away to safety. It was the bones that let Lion fly high in the sky. When Bullfrog broke the magic bones, the spell broke, too. Lion had to walk a long way back to his den.

The two very muddy white crows were sitting outside Lion's den. They were afraid that Lion would drop on them from the sky. The crows were so surprised to see Lion walking that they forgot about being scared.

"Bullfrog broke the bones!" they cried. "He said you could hunt for him at the dam."

Lion did not answer. He just pounced at them, ready to bite off their heads. Without thinking, the crows flew up in the air. When they realized that Lion could not follow, they laughed and said: "Lion cannot get us. We're free as birds."

Lion roared in anger. He dug in the cave until he found the one bone that Bullfrog had missed. It was a tiny bone from a warthog's foot, and its magic allowed the crows to talk. Lion snapped it between his teeth, and the crows said "Caw, caw."

Lion took off his wings and learned how to stalk his prey. When he was not hunting for food, Lion stalked Bullfrog. Every time Bullfrog heard Lion coming, he laughed and dived to the bottom of the water. Lion would sit on the bank and roar, but it did not change anything. Circles spread out on the water from where Bullfrog jumped. The circles reminded Lion of circling in the sky and made him even angrier.

Discussion Questions:

1. What did Lion do to keep his bones safe?

2. How did the little bullfrog outsmart the mighty lion?

3. Why were the crows safe at the end of the story?

4. If you could fly, where would you go and what would you do?

5. Choose an African animal. Think of a power that might change that animal as being able to fly changed the lion. Draw a picture of your magic animal.

Legends of Africa *(cont.)*

The Curious Monkey

Long ago, Dog was sleeping in the ashes of a fire in the middle of the forest. It was dark and shady there. Because this was the very first dog in the world, no one knew whether he was a good dog or a bad dog. All he did was sleep. Monkey was the first one to see Dog. Monkey had never seen anything like Dog before since this was the first dog in the world. Monkey could not keep a secret, so he went to tell the world.

All the animals came to see this new creature. "Here it is," said Monkey. "Does anyone know who this is?"

Elephant leaned over and looked with elephant eyes. "It is not an elephant," she said.

Okapi stepped up, bent her neck, and swung her head with okapi eyes back and forth over sleeping Dog. "This is not a giraffe or an okapi."

Next came scaly Anteater. He looked at the sleeping dog in his very slow way. He looked for a long time with anteater eyes and then he sat and went to sleep.

One by one Monkey asked the beasts to come and look at sleeping Dog but not one of them claimed sleeping Dog.

Finally Tortoise, who had been there for a very long time and who knew almost everything, called to Monkey from the tree where she was sitting. "Are you done asking?"

"Just about," answered Monkey. "We still do not know what this thing is or what it does!"

"Until you can think of a better name," said Tortoise, "I think you should call him 'Dog.' That is what he looks like to me."

Hearing his name woke up sleeping Dog, and he was angry. He opened his big dog eyes and looked at the animals all around him. "Who woke me up?" he asked. "I'll get you all!"

With that Dog charged at everyone, barking and showing off his big, strong, dog teeth. The animals ran away, and Dog followed them, planning to kill them all. Tortoise only laughed and pulled her head into her house. "You will never get me, Dog. But from this day forward you will chase any beast your dog eyes see." That is how it is, even today.

Discussion Questions:

1. Why did Tortoise stay when all the other animals ran away?
2. What do you think might have happened if an animal like a lion had been in the group?

Art
of
Africa

Background Information

African art extends from ancient times to the present day. The oldest works of art are rock painting and engraving that dates to 6000 B.C. African art reflects the cultural diversity of the continent's ethnic groups and gives expression to the rich histories, philosophies, religions, and societies of the people. Among the traditional types of African art are sculpture, furniture, pottery, textiles, and jewelry.

Each individual ethnic group has its own traditions regarding both the subject and form of representation. Some cultures value naturalistic representations while others favor abstraction. Materials used in art are determined by their availability in each region and include wood, fiber, metal, ivory, clay, earth, and stone.

Fiber Art

The Africans' love of color, patterns, and textures extends to almost everything used in daily life. In the rain forest, bark is harvested from trees, soaked, and beaten to form fabric for clothing. The Mbuti women use dyes extracted from other plants to paint and decorate each sheet. Elsewhere, fibers are stripped, dyed, and woven into cloth. The people of ancient Egypt wove the fibers of the flax plant into fine white cloth called linen. Kente, a highly decorative ceremonial fabric from Ghana, was originally made from raffia, like the baskets that inspired it. Later, silk was used to create a fine fabric. Kente cloth is made on a loom in long strips 4" (10.16 cm) wide. The strips are then woven together. Each of the many complex patterns has a name that reflects its symbolic meaning.

Metalwork

Metals, especially gold, iron, and bronze, are among the many natural resources of Africa. In ancient Egypt, gold was pounded into sheets and applied to furniture for the Pharaohs. Some of the elaborate golden masks, jewelry, and other items used by the Pharaohs have been recovered and preserved. They may be seen in museums around the world. The Asante are famous for their gold jewelry and other ornaments. For many generations, the gold mines of western Africa provided precious metal for trade and artworks. The quest for gold and other mineral riches led to the exploration and colonization of Africa by Asians and Europeans.

Archaeologists have found evidence that as early as 300 B.C. the people south of the Sahara desert produced iron. The ore was heated in furnaces made of earthenware and forged by smiths into different implements.

Background Information *(cont.)*

Metal work *(cont.)*

Artisans in Benin used a combination of copper, tin, lead, and zinc to create extraordinary bronze plaques and figures. They used the lost-wax process, similar to that used by the Asante. In this process, the artist first creates the shape of the object in loamy soil. Once it has dried, a smooth coat of beeswax is applied, and details are applied and/or etched. The piece is then covered with three layers of the same loamy soil and allowed to dry before it is fired. As the object is heated, the wax melts and runs out, leaving a space between the layers. The piece is then inverted in sand, and molten bronze is poured into the mold where it fills the space left by the melting wax. When the object has cooled completely, the artist removes all of the loamy soil, leaving only the delicate bronze figure.

Jewelry of Africa

Jewelry plays an important role in the cultures of Africa. Across the continent, women, men, and children adorn their bodies with beautiful jewelry of many different designs. Jewelry is worn on various parts of the body for decoration and carries special meanings in each society. Some jewelry is worn only on special occasions such as weddings and life-stage initiations. Other pieces are given as gifts, such as friendship bracelets. Rings, necklaces, armbands, ankle bracelets, earrings, bracelets, and hair ornaments can show the wealth and status of the wearer.

The traditional materials used for jewelry include fur, feathers, leather, claws, animal bones and teeth, shells, ivory, glass, and metal. The metals most commonly used for jewelry are gold, tin, copper, aluminum, and silver. Bronze, iron, and lead have also been used for jewelry.

Masks

The African people often use masks as part of their celebrations. The masks are made from a variety of materials and range from simple designs to ornate wood carvings. The subject may be an animal or a mythical being. Many people in other countries collect these masks as works of art.

132

Make a Woven Bag

In Morocco the women weave blankets, rugs, pillows, and bags. Complete the woven pattern on the blank half of the page. Fold your bag and tape or glue the sides together as shown. Punch a hole at the top of each side of the bag. Thread yarn or string through the holes. Tie a bow to close the bag.

Weaving with paper

Most Africans weave their cloth on a loom. Thread or yarn is passed over and under the woof, a series of threads that support the fabric. Here is one technique that can be used in weaving. Have students make woven paper as colorful as possible. (**Note:** Some students may need assistance with measuring, cutting, and weaving. Enlist the help of parent volunteers or older students as needed.)

Materials

- ruler
- scissors
- glue
- 2 pieces of 12" x 18" (30 cm x 46 cm) construction paper
- pencils

Directions

1. Cut one piece of construction paper into 1" (1.25 cm) and ¼" (.6 cm) wide strips.

2. Measure one inch (2.5 cm) from the top edge of the other piece of construction paper and draw a line. Fold the sheet of paper in half.

3. Turn the paper sideways and measure and draw equally spaced ½" (1.25 cm) lines.

4. Cut along the ruled lines. Do not cut through the top margin. This is a loom.

5. Select a ½" (1.25 cm) strip and begin weaving it under and over. Each strip is a weft. Take a second strip in another color and reverse the weaving, going over and then under.

6. Repeat the above steps until the the loom is filled.

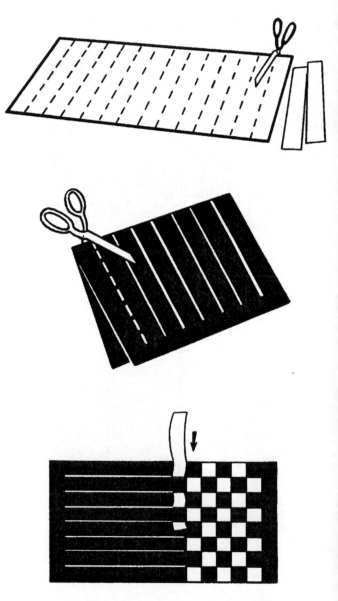

Extending the Activity

To make more complex patterns, begin by over-weaving the weft. Select a ¼" (.6 cm) strip and weave it under and over each weft strip in the same pattern, centering the narrow strips on the wider strips. After over-weaving, begin counter-weaving. With a strip, weave from the top to the bottom of the piece, going under and over the counter-weaving strips. Adjust the strips and use a small amount of glue to hold them in place. Trim the edges or let the ends extend in a fringe. Does your pattern have a name?

Folk Designs of Africa Bookmark

To make your bookmark, you will need an 8" x 2" (20.5 x 5 cm) strip of construction paper, crayons or markers, scissors, glue, a copy of the designs below and on page 136, and a pencil or pen.

Directions

1. Color and cut out one or more of these traditional African folk art designs.

2. Glue the designs on the strip of paper.

3. Write your name on the back of the bookmark.

4. To make your bookmark last longer, you can cover both sides of the strip with clear adhesive paper.

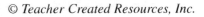

Folk Designs of
Africa Bookmark *(cont.)*

Make a Shell Picture

In Senegal some paintings are formed from small seashells. Look at the sample painting. Design your own seashell painting using dots and circles.

Necklace of King Tut

Pharaoh Tutankhamen lived in ancient Egypt. He was buried in a pyramid with many treasures. Color the necklace and cut the pattern on the dotted line. To wear the necklace, punch a hole in the tip of each wing and thread string through it.

138

Beads of Every Color and Shape

In Africa beaded jewelry has been popular for thousands of years. Children and adults often wear beaded jewelry such as armbands, headdresses, earrings, headbands, belts, and hair ornaments. Beads may be made from wood, glass, metal, clay, seeds, animal bones, precious stones, or plastic. Some beaded jewelry is worn for decoration and beauty. In some countries the colors, patterns, and even the number of beaded necklaces tells something about the person wearing them. Glass beads were once used as currency in some regions of Africa. You can make your own beaded jewelry to wear. The directions below show two ways to make your own beads. You can also use any beads, macaroni, buttons, pieces of cereal, or pieces of drinking straws.

Clay Beads on a String

Materials

- self-hardening clay
- paint or markers
- yarn or string
- plastic knife
- toothpick

Directions

1. Roll a ball of clay into a long "noodle" shape.
2. Cut the clay into small pieces.
3. Roll the clay pieces into round, oval, or square beads.
4. Make textures and patterns on the clay beads.
5. Use a toothpick to poke a small hole through the center of each bead.
6. After the beads are dry, decorate them with paint or markers. Thread the clay beads on a piece of string or pipe cleaner.

Paper and Metallic Beads

Materials

- wrapping paper
- aluminum foil or colorful pages from magazines
- clear tape
- string

Directions

1. Cut the paper or foil into small triangle shapes.
2. Begin at one side of the triangle and roll the paper into cylinder-shaped beads.
3. Tape the end of the triangle to seal the bead.
4. Thread your beads onto a piece of string.

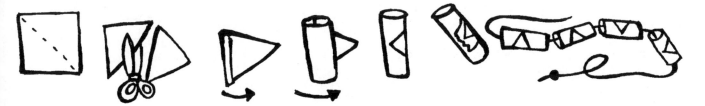

Make an African Mask

Masks are a very important part of African culture. Each mask has its own purpose. Some are worn as ornaments while others are used in religious ceremonies. Dancers wear them to communicate with spirits. The spirits express themselves through the masks. African masks are made of many different kinds of materials. They are decorated with simple, strong, and powerful shapes and designs. Doctors wear the masks to concentrate the healing powers of nature.

Have students make their own masks using the materials and directions below and on pages 141 and 142.

Materials

- brown, gray, black, or beige construction paper (for decorating mask)

- two 8" x 11" (20 cm x 28 cm) sheets of white construction paper per student (for mask pattern)

- pencils

- scissors

- glue or stapler

- patterns on pages 141 and 142

- *optional*: raffia or shredded husks

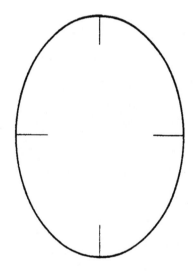

Directions

1. Reproduce the patterns on pages 141 and 142 onto white construction paper.

2. Have students cut out the top and bottom patterns of the mask. Cut the slits for the forehead, chin, and cheeks.

3. Overlap the sides of each slit and staple or glue them back together to create a three-dimensional effect.

4. Have students cut out geometric shapes to create the facial features and other designs for the mask. The eyes, nose, and mouth should be exaggerated to show their importance.

5. If desired, use raffia fibers or shredded cornhusks for hair.

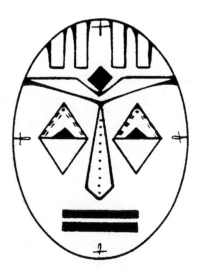

Make an African Mask *(cont.)*

Mask Pattern (Top)

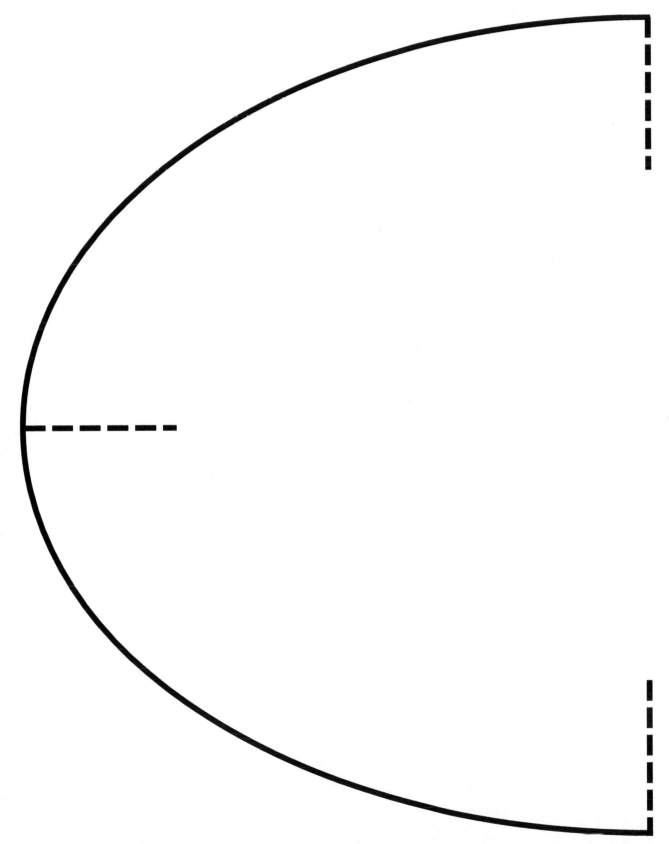

Make an African Mask *(cont.)*

Mask Pattern (Bottom)

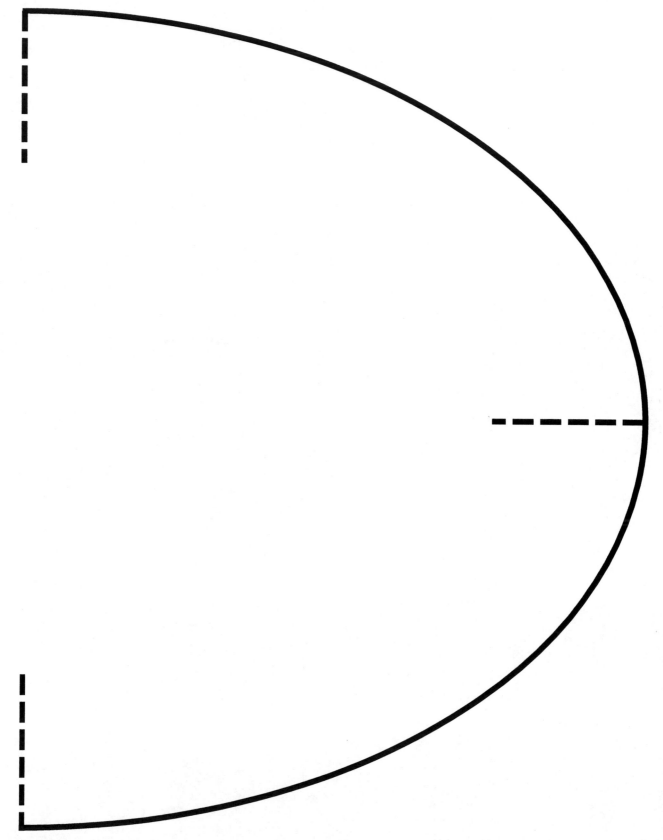

Games

and

Toys of

Africa

Background Information

Just like children everywhere, African children like to play with toys and share games. Some games that the children play help them learn counting, singing, storytelling, cooperation, competition and adult activities such as farming. Other games are played just for fun. Some of these games are thousands of years old, such as the Egyptian board game known as Mankala.

Board Games

The board game most often called Mankala is thousands of years old. There are countless variations that increase the difficulty of the game, and different names are used in different countries. Perhaps it was first played by scratching holes in the dirt. The object is to capture all of the opponent's playing pieces as the players move around the board. More sophisticated rules call for increasing game strategies in order to be successful.

Ball Games

Catch, kickball, tennis, basketball, and soccer are some of the games played with balls. In the rain forest children sometimes make kickballs from rubber found in the sap of the rubber trees.

String Games

Many children and adults know string games that are similar to "cat's cradle." Songs and legendary stories may be recited as the string patterns change.

Toys

Children buy dolls and toys at the market or fashion their own. To make their own toys, children often use wood, fur, animal hide, beads, shells, rocks, sticks, metal, feathers, and clay. Small toy animals can also be made from clay and woven grasses.

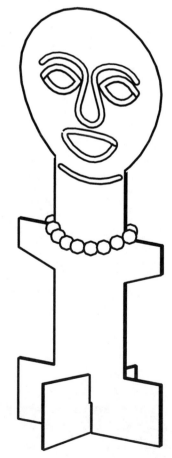

Dolls can also have other symbolic values for African girls and women. An Akua-ba doll expresses the hope that the individual will have children. A woman who loses a child, especially one of twins, often wears a doll pinned to her clothing to represent the lost child.

Group Games

Children play hopscotch, tag, jump rope, follow the leader, hide and seek, and riddle guessing games. Some children hold running and jumping contests. Children also enjoy clapping games and circle games where they might sing a familiar song or pretend to be magical beings.

African Games

Ta Mbele

This game is similar to Simon Says. Ta Mbele is a game played in the Congo. There it is played usually with just girls or just boys, but this way is only by their choice. It does not have to be played in this manner.

Playing the Game

Make a line down the center of the playing area, room, or playground, using masking tape or chalk. Children should be divided into two groups. Line up the children opposite each other about three to four feet from the line. A leader is chosen. The leader dances up and down between the groups while everyone is chanting "Ta Mbele." The leader dances and suddenly stops in front of one person and quickly extends a hand. The chosen person must extend the same hand at the same time. The object of the game is to match the leader's choice of left or right hand. If hands match, this person becomes the new leader. If there is no match, the leader takes another turn.

Bokwele

Bokwele is a great tag game that originated in the Congo. This game is pronounced "bok-Wee-lee." This game is played on a large playing field that has been divided into two equal halves.

Playing the Game

For this game you will need small objects, such as stones, marbles, or buttons, and six or more players. Divide the players into two teams and assign a side of the field to each team. Each team marks a circle on the ground about 6 feet (1.8 m) wide on its side of the field. Give each team a different set of small objects. For example, one team may be given a set of marbles and the other team, a set of buttons. It does not matter how many objects are in the sets as long as they are equal in size. The teams place their objects in their circles. The object of the game is to steal all of the items from the other team's circle and carry them back to your side of the field without getting tagged. If a player is tagged on the enemy's side of the field, he or she must return the stolen items to the other team's circle. The players are not allowed to stand guard over their circles. One team wins when it has stolen all of the opponent's objects, or the game may be played for a predetermined amount of time, in which case the team with the most objects would win.

African Games *(cont.)*

Yoté

Yoté is a popular game predominantly played in West Africa. Pebbles and sticks are used to play this outdoor game.

Playing the Game

Create a Yoté board by digging 30 small holes (six columns and five rows) into the dirt or sand. Each player begins with 12 markers. One player uses pebbles, and the other player uses small pieces of a stick. The game begins when the holder of the rocks places one rock into any hole. The stick player then places a stick into any open hole. Only one marker may be played per turn. A player is not required to put all of his or her markers around the Yoté board. At any time a player may choose to move one of his or her previously placed markers. These markers may only move one space up, down, left, or right and only into an empty hole. A player may capture an opposing marker (remove it from play) by passing a marker over it and into an empty hole. The capturing player is then allowed a bonus capture, removing from play an additional opposing marker from the board. The winner is the first player to capture all of his or her opponent's markers. However, the game may be called a draw if both players have three or fewer markers remaining on the board.

Achi

This game is played by the children of Ghana.

Playing the Game

To play this game, you will need eight game pieces (coins, pebbles, beans, etc.) and two players. Before the game can begin, the players need to draw a game board, using the diagram below. Each player begins with four game pieces. The players take turns placing one piece at a time onto an empty point anywhere on the game board. When all eight game pieces are on the board, the players will take turns moving one piece at a time along a line to an empty point. The object is for a player to get three of his or her pieces in a row. The first player to do so is the winner.

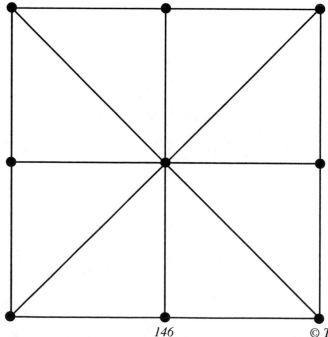

African Games *(cont.)*

=== **Wari** ===

Wari is a popular game in Africa, Asia, and the Middle East.

Playing the Game

To play this game, the players need a game board and 48 counters (seeds, pebbles, shells, coins, buttons, etc.) of various shapes and colors. The game board is simply twelve round depressions. The depressions can be scooped out of sand or dirt for outdoor play, or you can use a set of cups or even an egg carton. The objective of the game is to capture more counters than your opponent.

To start the game, the two opponents sit facing one another on opposite sides of the board. Each player takes one of the two rows. All 48 counters should be placed in the 12 depressions so that there are four counters in each one. Choose which players will go first, and from then on, the players will alternate turns. The player going first begins by picking up the four counters from any hole in his or her row and sowing them (placing them), one by one, in a counterclockwise direction in the next four holes. The other player then takes the counters from any hole in his or her row and sows them, one by one, to the right. And so the game continues.

Depending on the location of the chosen compartment, the sowing process may or may not continue into the opponent's side of the board. If there are eleven or more counters in a compartment, the player will sow all the way around the board and come back to the starting point or further so that is possible to sow a depression twice during the same move. The hole that was emptied, however, cannot be filled in the same turn in which it was emptied. If this happens, one must skip over it and continue to sow beyond it.

To capture all of the counters in an opponent's compartment, the last counter sown must fall into an opponent's compartment where there are two or three counters. The player who has captured these counters removes all of them and puts them into his or her reservoir (just a hole in the ground or a container next to the player, designed to hold the captured counters). A jar may be used as a reservoir.

If, after you have made a capture, there are either two or three counters in the compartment immediately preceding it on your opponent's side of the board, you are allowed to capture these as well. If you can make this move, the same rule applies to the compartment preceding the one so long as it is on your opponent's side of the board and contains two or three counters.

The game is over when a player has no counters left in his or her row with which to make a move. However, a player is not allowed to intentionally set up this situation by capturing all of the opponent's pieces from all of his or her compartments in one turn or by making a small move between compartments on one's side when the player could have sown one or more pieces into his or her opponent's side. This is so the player has the honor of putting himself or herself out of the game by sowing his or her last available counter onto the opponent's side of the board.

After the game ends, the player who still has counters on the board takes them all off of the board and drops them in his or her reservoir. The number of counters in each player's reservoir is tallied, and the one with the most counters is the winner.

African Games *(cont.)*

▬ Mankala ▬

Arabs call this game Kalah. They took it to Africa where it has many different names. In East Africa, it is called Mankala. In West Africa it is called Owara. In South Africa it is known as Ohara. No matter which version of the game is used, you and your students will enjoy playing Mankala.

Preparing the Game

To play this game, you will need the following:

- clean egg carton
- tape or glue

- bean seeds
- two red markers per player

Look at the picture on this page. Build the game board by separating the top and bottom of the egg carton. Cut the top section in half and attach each half to a side of the bottom section, as shown in the illustration. Each of the two end cups becomes a player's cup where he or she collects beans (points). The player's cup is on his or her right.

Playing the Game

Have students pick a partner and sit across from each other. Tell them to put three beans in each of the twelve cups in the egg carton. Have students decide which player goes first. The first player picks out the beans in the cup immediately on his or her left. This player should then put his or her red marker in the empty cup. Going counterclockwise away from the red marker, have the first player place one bean in each cup until all three beans have been used.

Look in the cup opposite the cup where the last bean was dropped. Have the first player take those beans out and place them in the end cup to his or her right. These beans are now the first player's points. The second player can do the same thing that the first player just did by repeating the third and fourth steps. When it is the first player's turn again, he or she finds his or her red marker and takes the beans from the cup to the right. That player distributes those beans as described above. If there are no beans in the cup to the right, that players puts his or her red marker into the empty cup, and it becomes the other player's turn. It is important to remember to move the red marker so that you know which cup to start with for your next move.

Continue to play until there is only one bean left. The last player to put any beans in his or her end cup gets the last bean. Both players count their beans. The player with the greatest number of beans in his or her cup wins the game.

African Games *(cont.)*

Bean Bowl

The Bean Bowl is a toss game that is played throughout the northern region of Western Africa. This is a great game for improving motor skills and counting skills while having lots of fun.

Playing the Game

To begin this game, place a bowl in a designated area in the room or outside. Measure a distance away from the bowl that is age appropriate for your students and mark it with a strip of masking tape. Give each player a cup with the same number of beans in it. Players take turns aiming and tossing the beans into the bowl and then counting how many went in. After all players have had a turn, the one who lands the most beans in the bowl wins. Variations could include having two teams, two bowls, and playing the game like a relay. The team with the most beans in the bowl wins.

Hide the Pebble

This popular traditional game is similar to "hide the button." It may be played on a wooden game board or by digging small holes in the ground and then filling them with sand. You can play this game in the classroom or on the playground. You will need an egg carton, paints or crayons, scissors, sand, and a pebble or marker.

Playing the Game

Children may work in pairs or groups of three. Cut the egg carton into three sections. Decorate the egg carton sections. Fill the holes in the egg carton with sand.

Playing Rules

One player hides the pebble in one of the sand-filled holes, using his or her hand to shield what he or she is doing. The second player tries to guess where the pebble is buried. Take turns hiding the pebble in the sand. Keep track of your correct guesses on your score sheet.

Score Sheet

Players			Correct Guess						

African Toy

Akua-ba Doll

The Aku-ba doll is a special doll made by the Ashante people of Ghana. This doll is carried by girls who hope to have children in the future and by women who hope that their children will be healthy and beautiful.

Materials

- cardboard sheet (one for each student)
- cardstock or poster board (for doll patterns)
- 3' (1m) thick yarn (any color)
- brown and black tempera paint
- bowl
- glue
- tape
- paintbrushes
- sharp scissors or mat knife (to be used by adults only)
- patterns on pages 151 and 152

Preparation

Trace the patterns from pages 151 and 152 on cardstock or poster board and cut them out to create templates for the dolls. Make one or more, depending on the number of students.

Directions

1. Demonstrate how to tape the templates to the cardboard square and trace the outline of each piece.

2. After each student has traced the patterns, have an adult cut the pieces from the cardboard using sharp scissors or a mat knife. It is helpful to place a cutting board beneath to protect the tabletop.

3. In a bowl, mix the black and brown tempera paint together to achieve the desired skin tone for your doll. Cover the workspace with newspapers. Place the cardboard patterns on the newspaper and paint one side. When they are dry, paint the other side of each.

4. Cut pieces of yarn to form the facial features of the doll. When you have decided on the placement of features, apply glue to the facial lines. Press the yarn down on top of the glue. Allow time to thoroughly dry.

5. Fit the entire body into the slot at the bottom of the doll.

6. Decorate your Akua-ba doll with beads around the neck and waist.

7. Set up a display with all the Akua-ba dolls. Bring in (or make) other dolls from different countries and cultures to compare.

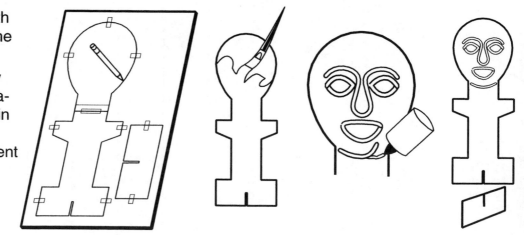

Africa Toy (cont.)

Akua-ba Doll

Head Pattern

Africa Toy *(cont.)*
Akua-ba Doll

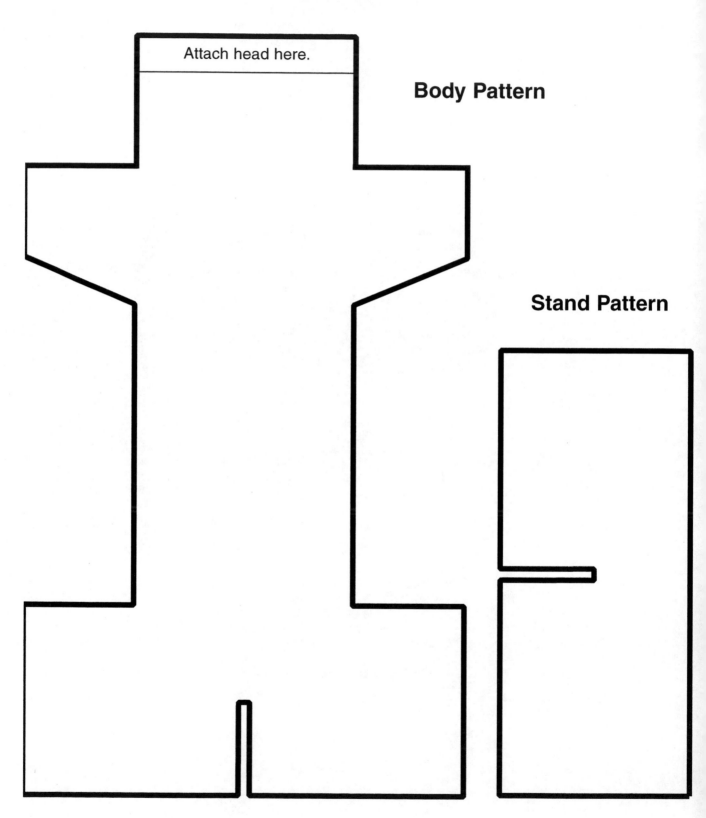

Attach head here.

Body Pattern

Stand Pattern

Music

of

Africa

Background Information

Music is an integral part of African life. It is used to teach values and to share knowledge. It plays an important role in communal and personal celebrations. Important stages of an African person's life are often marked with music. There are lullabies, children's game songs, music for adolescent initiation rites, weddings, title-taking ceremonies, funerals, and ceremonies for the ancestors. Speech, dance, and the visual arts often accompany music. The audience members often participate in a musical event by singing along with the chorus or by adding a rhythmic clapping pattern.

Music is also used to organize work activities. In Liberia, men clearing brush use a form of vocal hocketting, a pattern in which each person contributes a single note in strict sequence, to coordinate their machete blows. In the central rain forest, singing and vocal cries help hunters coordinate their movements, and in southern Africa herders use flutes and other instruments to help control the movement of cattle.

Each region and each ethnic group has its own musical traditions, but there are some common traits, including repetition of a pattern and polyphony. In vocal music the chorus is often a fixed refrain that alternates with improvisation by a lead singer. American jazz and gospel music are based on rhythms that began in Africa.

The African people use a wide variety of materials to fashion instruments ranging from simple rattles to elaborately carved drums. Some of these instruments have exotic sounding names and unfamiliar shapes. Others, like the xylophone and banjo, are commonplace in America, where African slaves introduced them.

Africans use drums of all shapes and sizes. Some African drums are simple, made of a piece of skin stretched over a pot or a dried and hollowed gourd. Some, like the double headed hourglass shaped drum from western Africa, are meant to be carried. Others are almost as tall as the drummer.

Other common percussion instruments in African music include clap-sticks, bells, rattles, slit gongs, struck gourds, clay pots, stamping tubes, and xylophones.

The thumb piano is an instrument unique to Africa. Made of a series of metal or bamboo strips mounted on a sounding board with a box or gourd as a resonator, the free ends of the strips are plucked with thumbs or forefingers. Sometimes called the traveler's friend because of its easy portability, such instruments are used throughout Africa and have many different names, like mbira, kalimba, or likembe.

Bamboo, reeds, wood, clay, bones, and other materials are used throughout the sub-Saharan region to make flutes, and guinea-corn or sorghum stems are used in the savanna region of western Africa to make clarinets. Trumpets are made from animal horns or wood.

A variety of stringed instruments is also used in African music. The musical bow, a string stretched between two ends of a flexible stave, is especially important in the traditional music of southern African peoples, such as the San, Xhosa, and Zulu. The kora, a harp-lute, has twenty-one strings and is made from a gourd, a skin membrane, and strings.

Great Sounds of Africa

The sound of music can be heard all over the continent of Africa. Music is a very important part of African life. The people of Africa use all kinds of materials to make their wonderful music. Below are some popular African instruments. Read about each one. Find some books about the music of Africa and instruments used in the different regions of Africa. Listen to African music and see if you can identify the sounds of some of the instruments you studied.

Lya-llu

The lya-llu is a talking drum. It is a double-headed, hourglass-shaped drum. The drum heads are held together by a number of thongs running from one head to the other. The lya-llu is held under one arm and played with a hammer-shaped stick.

Agogo

The agogo is an instrument with double bells. These metal bells are mounted together on a single frame. To make bell sounds, the player strikes the bells with a stick.

Sekere

The sekere is a gourd rattle filled with seeds, beads, or other items. Gourds are hollowed out and dried. Gourds of a variety of shapes and sizes are used to make these instruments. The gourd rattle is surrounded by nets of various see shells or beads.

Balaphon or Xylophone

This instrument is made from a set of wooden slabs joined together by bark-cords. The wooden slabs are set over a number of gourd resonators. These resonators help produce the sounds. Because they are different sizes, the resonators help the instrument to make different pitches. The keys (wooden slabs) are struck with mallet sticks.

Make Your Own Musical Instruments

You can make musical instruments to represent some of the instruments used in the countries of Africa. Collect the materials listed and follow the directions for each instrument. When you have finished making your instruments, gather some friends around and try playing some African music of your own.

Rattle

Materials

- paper tube from bathroom tissue
- paints or crayons
- dry rice or dry beans
- masking tape
- heavy paper
- scissors
- pencil

Directions

1. Decorate the paper tube with African designs. If you use paint, be sure the paint dries before moving on to the next step.
2. Place one of the open ends on a piece of heavy paper, and trace the circle shape of the tube onto the paper. Do this once more so you have two circles.
3. Cut out the circles.
4. Close up one of the tube ends by taping one of the circles to it.
5. Scoop some dry rice or dry beans into the tube.
6. Seal the other tube end as you did in Step 4.
7. Shake your new instrument to make the rattle sound heard in some African music.

Stick Shaker

This instrument makes an interesting sound when played along with drums, rattles, and stringed instruments.

Materials

- forked branch
- three to five buttons (Metal buttons with two or four holes work best.)
- thread
- scissors

Directions

1. Choose a forked branch that is not too big or heavy. One that fits comfortably in your hand works best. Break off any small branches that will be in the way as you play the shaker.

Make Your Own
Musical Instruments *(cont.)*

Stick Shaker *(cont.)*

Directions *(cont.)*

2. Cut the thread to a length of about three feet (one meter). Double or triple it to make the thread stronger.

3. Tie one end of the thread to a fork in the branch, as shown.

4. Thread three to five buttons through the free end of the thread.

5. Tie the free end of the thread to the other fork of the branch. The thread should be tight but not so tight that it will break.

6. Now, enjoy the shake, shake, shake, sound of your new instrument.

Drums

African music has special rhythms created by mixing different patterns of beats played on instruments such as the drum. The drum is the most important instrument in African music. Animal skins are used to make some drums. Other drums are made of hollow logs that are beaten with a stick. Follow the directions below to make a drum. When you have finished, use your hands to tap some African rhythms.

Materials

- coffee can with plastic lid
- can opener
- construction paper
- crayons, paints, or markers
- scissors
- glue

Directions

1. Ask an adult to use a can opener to remove the top and bottom of the coffee can. (By removing the bottom of the coffee can drum, you will be able to make a better sound.)

2. Cut a piece of construction paper that measures the length and width of the can (the cylinder).

3. Use crayons, paints, or markers to decorate the construction paper with colorful African designs.

4. Glue the construction paper to the outside of the coffee can cylinder.

5. Place the plastic lid on the top of the coffee can.

6. Listen to the drum beat of some African music. When you think you hear the beat or feel the rhythm, play your African drum along with the music.

My Book of Africa from A to Z

Make a Minibook About Africa

Follow these directions to make your own book of interesting facts about Africa.

1. Cut out the book pages.

2. Color the pictures on each page.

3. Arrange the pages in alphabetical order.

4. To finish your minibook, staple the pages. Share your book with your family and friends.

A Is for Africa

Africa A to Z Minibook

Name _____

My Book of Africa from A to Z *(cont.)*

Aa _____

A is for Africa.

Africa is one of the great continents. It is the second largest in the world. This continent is one of the most diverse with many different nationalities of people, religions, and customs.

Bb _____

B is for braids.

Many African girls braid their hair. The braids are arranged in unique styles. Beads are often used to adorn these lovely braids.

Cc _____

C is for civilization.

Africa is called the cradle of civilization.

In ancient Africa, there were great kingdoms like Egypt and Ethiopia. These countries had rich cultures and great universities long before other countries.

Dd _____

D is for drums.

A variety of instruments are used in Africa, but the drum is the most powerful. People dance to many different drumbeats. Drums make music and also announce special meetings.

My Book of Africa from A to Z *(cont.)*

Ee

E is for Egypt.

The early people of Egypt had a highly developed culture. They created great works of art, outstanding structures like the pyramids, and a form of picture-writing called hieroglyphics.

Ff

F is for family.

Africans are very warm people who take great pride in the family. They embrace a lot to show their joy, happiness, and support for one another. Often grandparents, parents and children all live together.

Gg

G is for grandparents.

Grandparents pass cultural ideas and traditions down the family lines. They tell wonderful stories to the children. They are said to be old and wise and that makes them beautiful too.

Hh

H is for horse.

Across northern Africa, horses are valued for their beauty and power. Horses are a symbol of wealth and power for their owners.

My Book of Africa from A to Z *(cont.)*

Ii _____

I is for ivory.

Elephants have ivory tusks. In the past ivory was traded in Africa. Now the elephants are protected from ivory hunters.

Jj _____

J is for jungle.

The jungle is home to a great variety of animals. The world's largest land animal, the elephant, and the world's tallest animal, the giraffe, live in the jungles of Africa.

My Book of Africa from A to Z *(cont.)*

Kk

K is for Kilamanjaro.

Kilamanjaro is the tallest mountain in Africa, rising over 19,000 feet. Even though this extinct volcano is near the equator, it has snow on top all year round.

Ll

L is for locust.

Locusts are flying insects and are found throughout the world. In Africa these pests travel in great swarms that may spread out for over 2,000 square miles. These locust swarms descend upon crops and trees, eating everything in sight.

My Book of Africa from A to Z (cont.)

M m

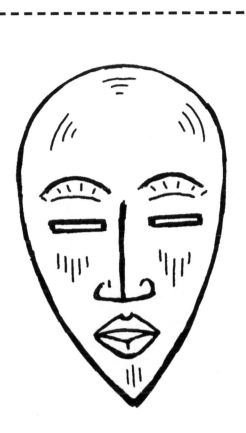

M is for mask.

Masks play an important role in many African cultures. Masks and costumes are used in masquerades. They are made to honor the spirits of ancestors and are brought out only for special occasions.

N n

N is for Nile.

The Nile River is the world's longest river. It flows from the Nile Valley in Egypt to the Mediterranean Sea. It stretches over 4,000 miles, and flows through Egypt, Uganda, Ethiopia, and Sudan.

Oo

O is for ornaments.

African people love to adorn their bodies with ornaments. Both men and women wear beads, bracelets, necklaces, hair dressings, earrings, and amulets.

Pp

P is for pyramid.

The great pyramids at Giza near Cairo, Egypt, were built about 2500 B.C. as tombs for some of the kings of ancient Egypt.

Qq

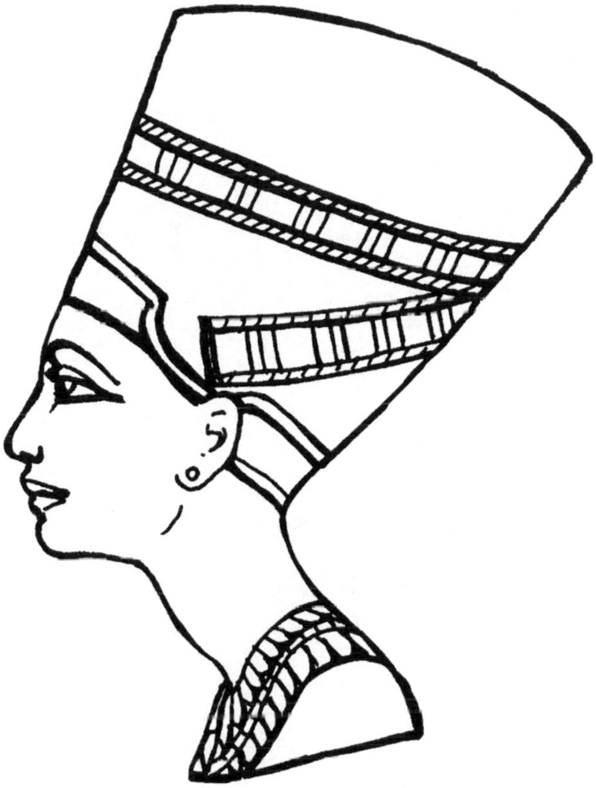

Q is for queen.

African queens wore their special crowns and splendid jewelry. In times past there were many kings and queens in Africa. Today, there are very few.

Rr

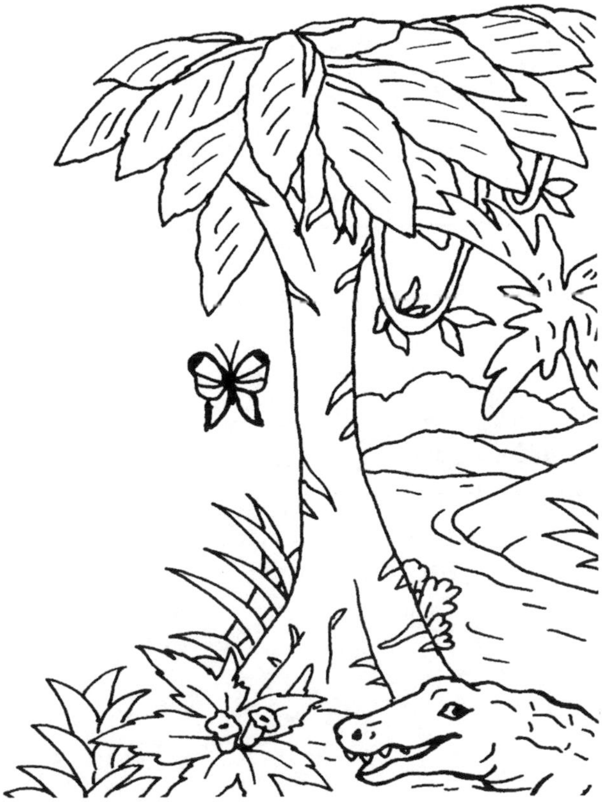

R is for rain forest.

The tropical rain forests of Africa are hot and humid. Tall trees with large leafy branches and other plants grow in the rain forest. Many animals make their homes in the rain forests.

My Book of Africa from A to Z *(cont.)*

Ss

- - - - - - - - - - -

SAHARA

S if for Sahara.

The Sahara is the world's largest desert. It is about the size of the United States. Thousands of years ago the Sahara was fertile and green. As time passed, rivers that once flowed in the area dried up. For this reason the Sahara is what it is today.

Tt

- - - - - - - - - - -

T is for Tuareg.

The Tuareg are Saharan nomads. They trade and travel in camel caravans and are known as the lords of the desert. The Tuareg refused to unite with other desert groups and remained independent. They raise camels and horses.

My Book of Africa from A to Z *(cont.)*

Uu _____

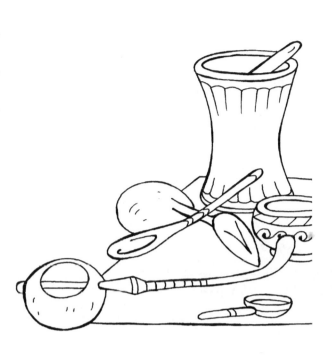

U is for utensils.

A variety of special utensils are used in Africa. Most utensils are made from wood or metal. Carved wooden spoons are used for cooking, for display in the home, and as symbols of status.

Vv _____

V is for village.

Many Africans live together in villages where they share similar beliefs and customs. Some extended families and clans build their homes in enclosed courtyards. The elders of each village teach the children the customs and legends of their clan.

Ww

W is for well.

Water is very precious in Africa. Wells are vital for the survival of rural villages. The women and girls go to the village wells every day. They carry water in a calabash, a watertight basket, or other containers.

Xx

X is for Xylophone.

The xylophone, or balaphon, is an African instrument. It is played by striking wooden slabs with a mallet.

My Book of Africa from A to Z *(cont.)*

Yy

Y is for Yoruba.

The Yoruba are farmers and traders who live in Nigeria. The Yoruba people are well known for their art, including masterpieces of woodcarving and bronze casting.

Zz

Z if for zebra.

There are two kinds of zebras that roam the African savannas. Burchell's zebras have black shadowed stripes. Grevy's zebras have thinner stripes. Every zebra has its own unique pattern of stripes. Zebras can identify each other by these patterns.

My Country Report

Use the following pages to write about and illustrate some of the interesting things you learned about a country in Africa. When you are finished, share your report with others.

Name _____

Country _____

Locate and color your African country on the map below.

On a piece of drawing paper, draw a map of your African country.

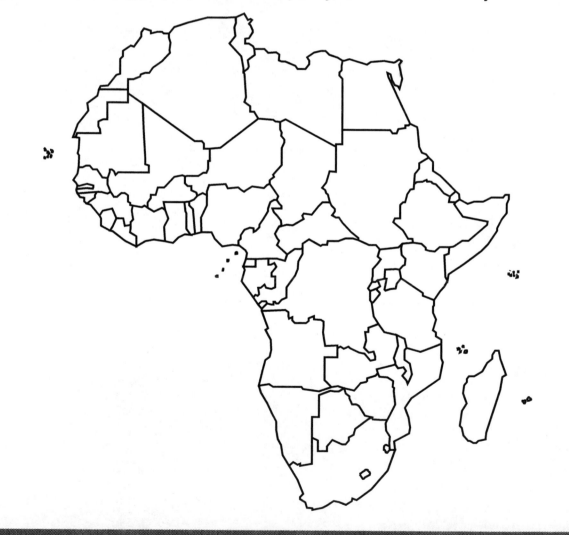

My Country Report *(cont.)*

Do some research to learn about the country you are studying. In the space below and on the following page, write the most interesting facts you learned about the clothing, animals, plants, art, music, food, and people of this country.

Clothing_____

_____

_____

_____

Animals _____

_____

_____

_____

Plants _____

_____

_____

_____

My Country Report (cont.)

Art _____

_____

_____

_____

Music_____

_____

_____

_____

Food _____

_____

_____

_____

People_____

_____

_____

_____

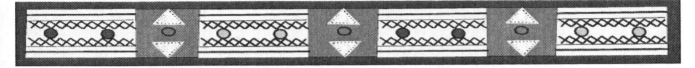

My Country Report *(cont.)*

Each country in Africa has its own flag. Each one is special. Use an encyclopedia or other reference book that has pictures of country flags in it. Find the flag of your African country. Use the space below to draw the flag. Be sure to match the colors in your drawing to the actual colors on the flag.

This is the flag of _____.

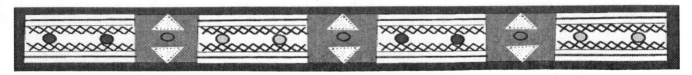

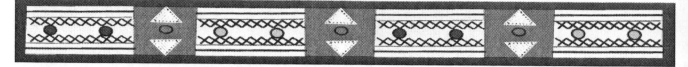

My Country Report *(cont.)*

Use the space below to write about the following:

1. The three most interesting facts I learned about this country are _____

_____

_____

_____

_____

_____

2. Think about whether or not you would like to live in this country. Write your

ideas on the lines below. Explain your answers. _____

_____

_____

_____

_____

_____

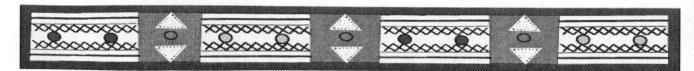